DAY TRIPS:
ST. LOUIS

Compiled by Carolyn Callison
Betty Taylor
Julie Blattner

Edited by Shifra Stein
Local maps by Joan Keiser

Shifra Stein's

DAY TRIPS
Gas-saving getaways less than two hours from GREATER
ST. LOUIS

HARPER & ROW, PUBLISHERS, New York

Cambridge, Philadelphia, San Francisco, London
Mexico City, São Paulo, Sydney

1817

Trademark registration pending for "Day Trips," application Serial No. 327,585.

FIRST EDITION

Designer: Ernie Haim

Library of Congress Cataloging in Publication Data

Stein, Shifra.
  Gas-saving getaways less than two hours from Greater St. Louis.

  (Shifra Stein's Day trips) (Harper colophon books; CN/902)
  I. Saint Louis region (Mo.)—Description and travel—Guidebooks. I. Callison, Carolyn. II. Taylor, Betty. III. Blattner, Julie. IV. Title. V. Series: Stein, Shifra. Day trips.
F474.S23S74   917.78′660443   81-48244
ISBN 0-06-090902-1 (pbk.)   AACR2

---

82 83 84 85 86 10 9 8 7 6 5 4 3 2 1

For those who love the rivers, hills, and backroads of Missouri and Illinois—especially Bob, Jason, and John

CONTENTS

INTRODUCTION

It took a while to uncover the vast amount of information about the area surrounding Greater St. Louis. We had a great deal of fun discovering places we never knew existed. There were backroads that weren't on any map, and they led us past elegant mansions, Ozark plateaus, river bluffs, and many wonderful historic sites—some of which date back as far as the eighteenth century.

Although we tried to be specific, in some cases towns were so small that no street addresses or phone numbers were listed for restaurants, hotels, or shops. Many sights are located off main highways, but we have included maps and extensive directions to aid you in your travels. The local people are also very helpful, so don't hesitate to ask for directions if you get lost.

We hope you enjoy taking day trips through Missouri and Illinois as much as we have. If you find any new spots you think should be included for future editions, please let us know.

Shifra Stein
c/o Harper & Row
10 East 53rd Street
New York, N.Y. 10022

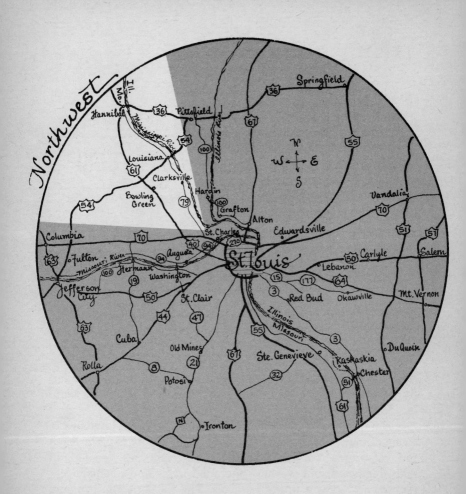

NORTHWEST

DAY TRIP I

Clarksville
Louisiana
Hannibal
Bowling Green

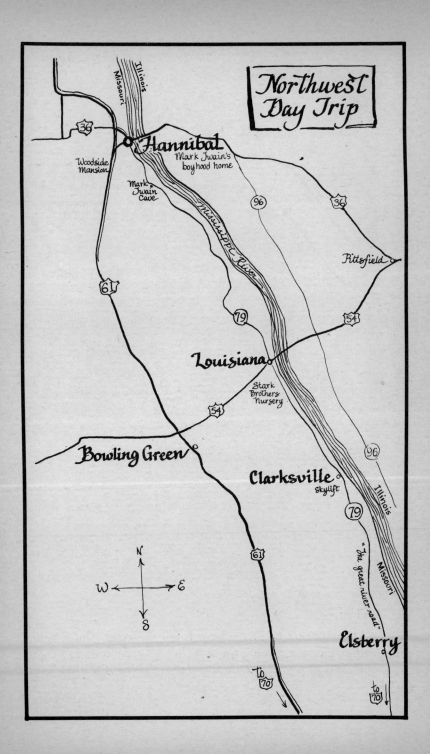

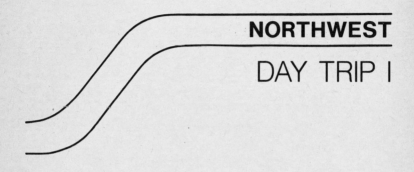

NORTHWEST

DAY TRIP I

CLARKSVILLE

The Great River Road runs along the banks of the Mississippi River for over 5,000 miles, from northern Minnesota to the state of Louisiana. This magnificent road stretches for 215 miles (346 km) in Missouri as M-79 and takes you past some of the state's most scenic landmarks.

Driving north from St. Louis on M-79, you'll arrive at the town of Clarksville, which is scattered over the highest and some of the most picturesque bluffs on the Mississippi. The settlement dates back to 1816 and it is said that William Clark (of Lewis and Clark fame) spent a winter here when he was serving as territorial governor prior to 1820. If you visit Clarksville around December, you may get a chance to see the bald eagles flying high above the river bluffs.

WHERE TO EAT

Duvall Restaurant. On M-79 across from the skylift. The restaurant offers clean surroundings and no-nonsense country cooking each day from early morning until evening. Call 314-242-9680.

LOUISIANA

A few miles north of Clarksville is Louisiana, a town that was once a river port, which had to turn to agriculture and industry to survive. First laid out in 1818 along the riverbank, the town extended inland as it grew. Named for the state, Louisiana is not particularly imposing on first glance, but as you drive through, you may find yourself admiring the array of antebellum and Victorian "gingerbread" homes.

WHERE TO GO

The Stark Brothers Nursery. Near Louisiana. It is one of the oldest and largest nurseries in the United States. It was founded by James Stark in 1816. The Red and Golden Delicious apples that we all know and love were first developed here. You can pick out your own fruit trees and other landscaping materials at the Garden Center. They don't, however, sell the fruit or vegetable products here—you have to grow your own. To find the Garden Center if you are driving north on M-79, turn left on Georgia Street at the second stop sign in Louisiana, and continue through the business district. Here you will pass many of the town's stately homes. The Garden Center is about 3 miles (4.8 km) from town. Just follow the signs. Call 314-754-3113.

WHERE TO EAT

Olde Hotel Restaurant. On 125 S. 3rd St. in Louisiana. Housed in the downstairs of this antebellum hotel, the restaurant has been in operation for 18 years. The Sunday special of turkey and dressing is so good that it attracts hungry travelers from all over the area. The Olde Hotel is open Monday through Friday 6 A.M. to 7 P.M.; Saturday and Sunday 6 A.M. to 3 P.M. Call 314-754-5411.

Li'l Henry's. 321 Mansion Drive. Junction U.S. 54, M-79, and the bridge. Try the fried river catfish at this popular lunch spot. The fried chicken and cocktails are also good. Open Sunday through Thursday 6 A.M. to 10 P.M.; on Friday and Saturday 6 A.M. to 11 P.M. Call 314-754-3116.

HANNIBAL

As you continue north along M-79, you'll reach Hannibal, best known as Mark Twain's hometown. This is the site where Samuel Clemens found the inspiration and characters for some of his best-loved books. Don't come here with great expectations of finding the ambling river town of Mark Twain's boyhood. Chances are he would take delight in satirizing the commercialization of this area today. (Next door to his boyhood home sits a drive-in fast-food restaurant.) But if you can overlook the "marketing" of his childhood stomping grounds, it is still fascinating to view some of the things the way Clemens saw them as an impressionable child. For more information, and hours, write the Hannibal Tourism Commission, 118 Hill Street, Hannibal, or call 314-221-2477.

Here are a few of the more interesting spots that are open to the public.

WHERE TO GO

Mark Twain Boyhood Home and Museum. 208 Hill Street. Twain's father built the house in 1843 and little Samuel lived here between the ages of 9 and 18. On display is a large collection of Twain mementoes, including several first editions and original manuscripts of his works. In addition, the museum houses a collection of 16 original Norman Rockwell oil paintings used to illustrate special editions of *Tom Sawyer* and

Huckleberry Finn. Call 314-221-9010. *Mark Twain Birthplace Shrine.* See p. 165.

Becky Thatcher House. 211 Hill Street. The parlor and bedroom have been restored to look as they did when Laura Hawkins (Becky's real-life model) lived here. Call 314-221-0822.

Mark Twain Cave. 2 miles (3.2 km) south of Hannibal on M-79. This is where the infamous Injun Joe died, and where Tom and Becky were lost. It is designated a United States Natural Landmark, and is also the oldest commercial cave in the state. Open Memorial Day through Labor Day 8 A.M. to 8 P.M. and 9 A.M. to 5 P.M. the rest of the year. Admission fee. Call 314-221-1656.

Mississippi Riverboat *Mark Twain.* Center Street Landing. This riverboat takes you on an hour-long cruise on the Mississippi. Excursions leave daily from 11 A.M. in the summer. In September and October there is one cruise only, leaving at 1:30 P.M. There is a charge for the cruise. Call 314-221-3222.

Rockliffe Mansion. 1000 Bird Street (15 minutes from the riverboat landing). Owned by lumber magnate John Cruikshank, who lived there from 1900 until his death in 1924, this Victorian mansion was unoccupied for 43 years. Its art nouveau decor has recently been restored and it is now open to visitors daily 9:30 A.M. to 5:30 P.M. Admission fee. Call 314-221-4140.

Garth Woodside Mansion. Route 1; proceed 1 mi (1.6 km) S. of Hannibal on U.S. 61, then ¾ mi (1.2 km) S. on Route 1. This 20-room country estate was built in 1871 by one of Twain's life-long friends. It contains seven Italian fireplace mantels and a "flying staircase" that seems to float to the third floor without visible means of support. Daily tours May through October 9:30 A.M. to 5:30 P.M.; November through April 11 A.M. to 4 P.M. Admission fee. Call 314-221-2789.

Unsinkable Molly Brown House. U.S. 36 at Denkler Alley. Margaret Tobin Brown, known as "Unsinkable Molly Brown," was another famous Hannibal resident. She is credited with saving the lives of many fellow passengers on the ill-fated ship *Titanic*, which sank in 1912. She was born in Hannibal and moved away to make her fortune in the Colorado silver lodes. Her childhood home has been restored to its 1875 elegance. Displays include her early days in Hannibal as well as documentation of her heroism aboard the *Titanic*. Closed November through April. Admission fee.

WHERE TO EAT

Ole Planter's Restaurant. 316 North Main Street. Lunch is served here from 11 A.M. to 4 P.M. Specialties are thick sandwiches, home-baked pies, and American-Italian dishes such as spaghetti and lasagna. A plate lunch sells for $2.35. The restaurant reopens 4:30 to 8 P.M. for dinner, with prices ranging from $3.50 to $7.50. The "gourmet specialties" include the Pork Delight, with melted cheese, mushrooms, choice of vegetable, salad bar, and French bread. Closed Sundays. Call 314-221-4410.

Mark Twain Dinette. Third and Hill Streets. Known for its enormous hamburgers, roast beef, and hearty country chicken dinners. Open daily 6 A.M. to 11 P.M. Call 314-221-5300.

SPECIAL EVENTS

Tom Sawyer Days Festival. Hannibal, Missouri. Each summer, the town hosts this festival in which aspiring "Tom Sawyers" compete in frog jumping and raft racing contests, along with other events based on the novel. Participants from each of the ten states bordering on the Mississippi take part in the proceedings, which culminate in the National Tom Sawyer Fence Painting Contest on July 4.

Autumn Folklife Festival. Hannibal, Missouri. Held each fall, usually the first weekend in November. The Hannibal Arts

Council presents this weekend festival that features traditional crafts, food, and music of the area. For information on exact times and dates, call the Hannibal Arts Council, 625A Broadway, 314-221-6545.

BOWLING GREEN

If you return from Hannibal by driving south on U.S. 61, you'll travel through fertile farmland. Smack in the middle of all the pretty scenery is Bowling Green. Located in Pike County, Bowling Green was first platted in 1826 and is named for the Kentucky home of many of the town's first settlers. Pike County itself was settled in 1808 and named for Brigadier General Zebulon Pike, who discovered the Colorado mountain peak that now bears his name.

One of Pike County's most distinguished citizens hails from Bowling Green: Hon. Champ Clark was the only Speaker of the U.S. House of Representatives who resided in Missouri. He named his home "Honey Shuck" after the many honey locust trees in his yard. The house, at 220 West Church Street, is being restored and furnished as it was when the Clark family lived there at the turn of the century. It is open from June through August on weekends 1:30 P.M. to 4:30 P.M. No admission fee.

WHERE TO EAT

Chums Restaurant. 30 miles (48.3 km) south of Bowling Green at U.S. 61 and M-47 in Troy. On your way home via U.S. 61, stop here for moderately priced generous servings of country cooking. The pork tenderloin sandwich is excellent, as are the American fries made from real (not frozen) potatoes. There's also a reasonably priced catfish dinner, plus homemade bread and rolls. The place is a favorite with truckers because it's open 24 hours a day, seven days a week. Call 314-528-6121.

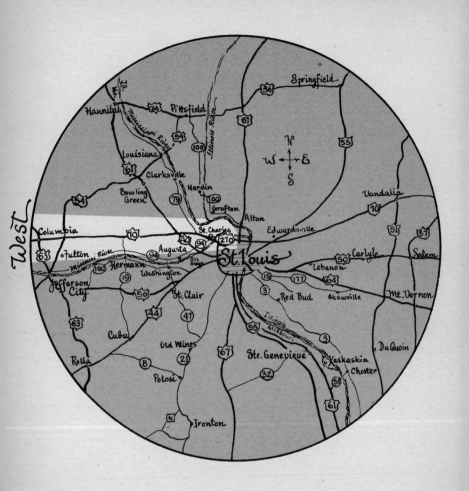

WEST
DAY TRIP I

St. Charles
Portage des Sioux

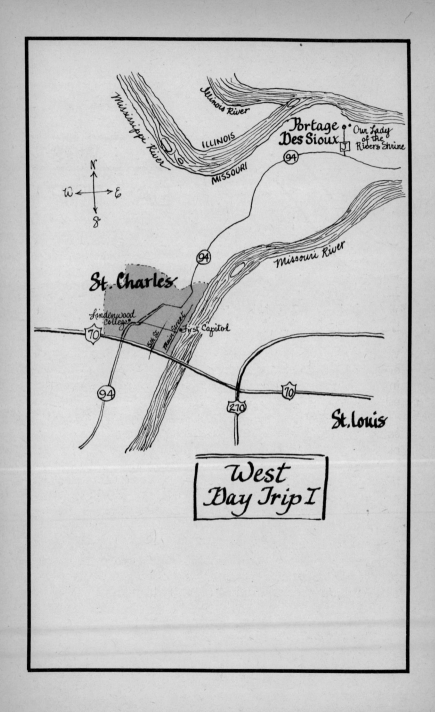

Mississippi River

Illinois River

ILLINOIS

MISSOURI

Portage
Des Sioux

⊙ Our Lady
of the
River's Shrine

94

N
W — E
S

94

Missouri River

St. Charles

Lindenwood
College

70

5th St.

Main Street

First Capitol

94

270

70

St. Louis

West
Day Trip I

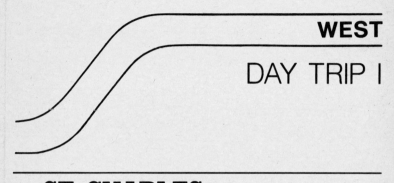

WEST

DAY TRIP I

ST. CHARLES

When St. Charles was first founded in 1769 by French fur trader Louis Blanchette, it was known as "Les Petites Côtes," meaning the little hills. As you drive up and down these hilly, picturesque streets you'll understand why.

It was later renamed San Carlos, in honor of the patron saint of King Charles IV of Spain. By 1804, it had been anglicized to St. Charles.

Located west of St. Louis on I-70, the town has played a major role in American's expansion west. The Lewis and Clark expedition stopped here in 1804, and when they returned nearly two and a half years later, the town gave them a rousing welcome.

St. Charles was the first state capital of Missouri and legislators met here from 1821 to 1826. The restored capitol is the focal point of the eight-block historic district, where you can explore dozens of shops full of crafts and antiques.

WHERE TO GO

St. Charles Visitor Information Center. 500 S. Riverside Drive.

The nice people in this center, located in the old Missouri-Kansas Train Depot in Frontier Park, will give you brochures on area attractions and fill you in on the history of the town. It should be your first stop. No admission fee. Call 314-946-7776 or 925-1776.

Missouri's First State Capitol. 208–216 South Main Street. From 1821 until 1826, the state legislature met here to make the formative decisions required of Missouri's government. The building has been restored and furnished as it was when the legislature met here. Open Memorial Day to Labor Day, Monday through Saturday 10 A.M. to 4 P.M., Sunday noon to 6 P.M.; for the rest of the year, Sunday noon to 5 P.M.

Newbill-McElhiney House Museum. 625 South Main Street. The St. Charles County Historical Society now owns this 1838 building and it has been refurnished to its nineteenth-century grandeur. Open Wednesday through Sunday 1 to 4 P.M. No admission fee. Call 314-723-2939.

Sibley Hall. Lindenwood College, Kingshighway and First Capitol Drive. Established in 1827, Lindenwood College is one of the oldest schools west of the Mississippi. Major George C. Sibley and his wife, Mary Easton Sibley, founded the school and built the original structure, Sibley Hall, which is now the central part of the campus. Tours by appointment only. Call 314-723-7152.

SHOPS

If you visit on Monday, you'll find many of these shops closed. Most are open on Sundays. There are two distinct shopping districts, one on South Main Street and one in "Frenchtown" on North Second Street.

FRENCHTOWN

Antiquity I. 1409 North Second Street. They've got oak furniture, glassware, sideboards, lamps, and desks. Call 314-724-1540.

Pitcher Corner Antiques. 1400 North Second Street. Lots of furniture, glassware, china, and lamps here. Open on weekends only, 10 A.M. to 5 P.M. Call 314-724-7609.

MAIN STREET

Lavender and Lace Antiques. 724 South Main Street. The eighteenth and nineteenth centuries are alive and well in this shop full of relics from those eras. Call 314-946-6899.

The Glass Workbench. 515 South Main Street. Beautiful leaded and stained-glass work. They also have a good stock of supplies for the do-it-yourselfer. Call 314-723-3557.

Grandma's Folly. 401 South Main Street. The perfect stop for unusual children's gifts—all handmade and adorable. Call 314-724-5656.

St. Charles Artist Guild. 524 South Main Street. You might discover next season's van Gogh here—or at least the perfect wall hanging for that bare spot above the piano. Local artists bring their work here for display and for sale.

Country House Furniture. 19 East Perry Street. Just off Main Street, this shop owner personally makes each piece to his own very exacting specifications. Handmade quality furniture is what he sells. Call 314-925-0066.

WHERE TO EAT

Aubuchon's. 614 South Main Street. A great place to take a break in your St. Charles tour. Sip an ice-cream soda (the creamy old-fashioned kind) or try a deli-style sandwich and some fresh-baked cookies. Open daily 11 A.M. to 6 P.M. Call 314-351-8457.

Copper Platter Restaurant. 625 South Main Street. You must try the homemade soups in the cozy atmosphere of this restaurant that is open for lunch only, Tuesday through Sunday 11 A.M. to 3 P.M. Call 314-925-0745.

Hob Nob Cafeteria. 108 South Main Street. If you are in a hurry, stop here for basic, home-cooked cafeteria fare. Open Monday through Friday 6:30 A.M. to 7 P.M.; Saturdays 6:30 A.M. to 2 P.M. Closed Sundays. Call 314-723-0320.

Pios Restaurant and Cocktail Lounge. 403 First Capitol Drive. Italian food and prime rib are the specialties here and the Italian-style salad is terrific. Open Monday through Saturday 10 A.M. to 1 P.M.; Sundays 3 P.M. to 10 P.M. Call 314-724-5919.

St. Charles Vintage House Restaurant and Wine Garden. 1219 South Main Street. When it is warm outside, you can eat lunch or dinner on the terraced garden overlooking the Missouri River. Open Tuesday through Saturday 11 A.M. to 10 P.M.; Sundays 10 A.M. to 8 P.M. The Sunday brunch buffet is served 10 A.M. to 1 P.M. Closed Mondays. Call 314-946-7155.

The Fudge Shop. 416 South Main Street. If your sweet tooth is nagging, stop here for some mouth-watering fudge. There is also a selection of doll houses, miniatures, and gifts for sale. Call 314-724-3961.

PORTAGE des SIOUX

To get here from St. Charles, follow M-94 east and turn north on County Road J. In 1763 this area belonged to the French. It was ceded to Spain in 1763 and then to Napoleon in 1800. The United States finally adopted it in 1803. The name evolved from a battle between the Sioux and Missouri Indian tribes. The Sioux used the area as an overland escape route to elude the Missouri Indians. The tiny village became a center of military operations during the War of 1812 and today it is a haven for area boat owners who find it a perfect spot for launching.

WHERE TO GO

Shrine of Our Lady of the Rivers. At the foot of LeSieur Street. In 1951, floodwaters from the rapidly rising Missouri River spilled onto the peninsula and joined with the Mississippi, thus isolating Portage des Sioux and threatening the residents with devastation. The townspeople prayed fervently that their tiny town be saved. It was. In gratitude for what they believed to be the answer to their prayers, they erected a statue to "Our Lady of the Rivers." The 27-foot fiberglass monument stands on a concrete peninsula, keeping watch over the river. After you read the historic markers on the walkway, stop for a picnic lunch at one of the riverside tables. Open daily, dawn to dusk. No admission fee. If you want your boat to have the church's blessing, join the annual "Blessing of the Fleet" procession held each July. The boats pass by the statue and receive a blessing given by a Catholic priest.

WEST

DAY TRIP II

Crane's Store
Fulton
Columbia

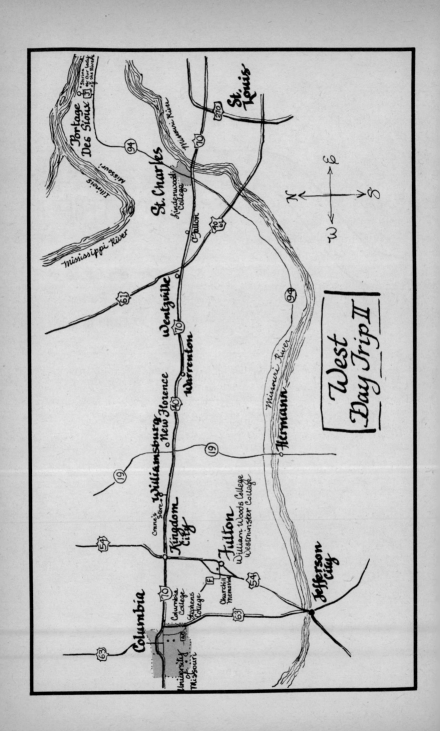

West
Day Trip II

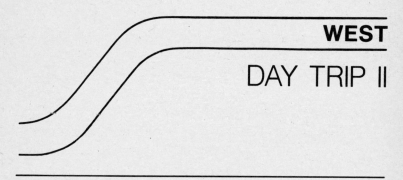

CRANE'S STORE

West of St. Charles, I-70 winds through St. Peters, O'Fallon, Wentzville, Foristell, Wright City, and Warrenton. As you near the New Florence/Hermann exit, it is hard to believe that the foothills of the Ozarks are barely out of sight (see Hermann, p. 37). Twelve miles (19.3 km) west at the Williamsburg exit, on the edge of the Loutre Valley's natural woodlands, is Crane's General Store.

This trading post has been in business for years, serving the Mineola and Shamrock settlements and providing a deserved break from tiresome travel over St. Charles Rock Road and early Highway 40 between St. Louis and Kansas City. Crane's still provides for the necessities of daily life, but the store has also become a veritable museum of toys and store items from days long past. Take time for a cool drink and hope that Bill Crane has time to point out some of his choicest collectibles to you. Call 314-254-3311.

FULTON

Back on I-70, continue to Kingdom City and the U.S. 54 exit to

Fulton, the county seat of Callaway County and site of Missouri State Hospital.

Fulton is probably best known as the home of Westminster College and William Woods College for Women. It was in Fulton, during the presidency of Harry S. Truman, that Sir Winston Churchill delivered his famous "Iron Curtain" speech in 1946. During the Kennedy presidency, it was proposed that the bombed-out remnant of London's St. Mary Aldermanbury Church be saved and reconstructed on American soil. Sir Winston immediately embraced the idea and the task of transporting and re-erecting the Christopher Wren masterpiece began. St. Mary Aldermanbury is now Westminster College's chapel and a place of worship for all, a symbol of history's debt to Churchill and the aspirations of people everywhere for dignity and freedom.

The undercroft of the church is a museum, gallery, and library for the study of Churchill's life, his blueprint for peace, and the six decades that bear the imprint of his mind and personality. Some examples of Wren's architecture are also included.

To reach the Churchill memorial, take County Road F exit off U.S. 54 and turn left on F to Westminster Avenue, then left again to the corner of Seventh Street. Hours daily from 9:45 A.M. Closed holidays. Special group and educational rates available. Admission fee. Call 314-642-6648.

COLUMBIA

At this point it would be a hard choice whether to travel south to Jefferson City and the Lake of the Ozarks, or to return via U.S. 54 to I-70 and on to Columbia. It all depends on your timetable and how you want to take your Day Trip. Columbia is a fun choice for a short trip.

Long established as a college town, Columbia is now being recognized as a travel destination in mid-Missouri. The University of Missouri was founded here in 1839 as the first state university west of the Mississippi, and shares Columbia with Columbia College (formerly Christian College) and Stephens College. Because Columbia is a university community, there are more than the usual number of travel attractions, including concerts, plays, and sports events.

The town's unique downtown shopping area is replete with boutiques carrying the newest merchandise from around the country. Because Columbia attracts so many visitors each year, it has excellent antiques shows and several better antiques shops.

With two public golf courses, 19 public tennis courts, and 36 public parks, compact Columbia has all the advantages of a large city and it makes it easy for you to enjoy your favorite sport.

Some other things to enjoy are:

MUSEUMS AND GALLERIES

Columbia Art League. 12 North Tenth Street. Shows are presented bimonthly. Hours: Monday through Saturday 10 A.M. to 3 P.M.; Sunday 3 A.M. to 5 P.M. Call 314-443-8838.

Columbia College Art Center. 1107 Broadway. Presents traveling exhibits monthly. Open weekdays 8 A.M. to 5 P.M.; Saturday 1 to 5 P.M. Sunday 2 to 5 P.M. Call 314-449-0531, ext. 368.

Columbia Gallery of Photography. 310 North Tenth Street. This is the only gallery in town devoted exclusively to photography. Open Monday through Saturday 9 A.M. to 5:30 P.M. Call 314-443-0503.

Stephens College Visitors Center Art Gallery. 1200 East Broadway. This unique solar-heated building contains the Maclanburg Gallery, which exhibits the Hinkhouse Collection of contemporary art, the Berman collection, and works of art by the late Albert Christ-Janer. Call 314-442-2211.

Wilbur R. Enns Entomology Museum. Hitt and Rollins streets, Agriculture Building, second floor. Over 1 million specimens, mostly from Missouri, are on display. Group tours by appointment. Open weekdays 9 to 11 A.M. and 2 to 4 P.M.. Call 314-882-2410.

Maplewood. M-63 and Route AC. The 1870 home of Frank G. Nifong is in the National Register of Historic Sites. It is open April through October, Sundays 2 to 5 P.M. or by appointment. Call 314-449-5876.

State Historical Society of Missouri. East end of Ellis Library on the University of Missouri campus. The Society has an extensive collection of Missouri newspapers and is most helpful in helping you find information. Visitors' parking across the street. Open Monday through Friday 8 A.M. to 4 P.M. Call 314-882-7083.

For more information, contact the Convention and Visitors Bureau, Columbia Chamber of Commerce, 32 North Eighth Street, P.O. Box 1016, Columbia, MO 65205, or call 314-874-1132.

WHERE TO GO

Live entertainment. Provided by the Maplewood Barn Theater (call 314-442-5717), M-63 and County Road AC (Nifong Park), and Stephens College Summer Dinner Theatre (call 314-442-2211, ext. 333). There are also theater offerings at Columbia College, Tenth and Rogers streets. Call 314-449-0531, ext. 370.

WHERE TO EAT

Haden House. 4515 Highway 63 north. This restored plantation home retains the setting and elegance it knew nearly 150 years ago. Specialties include hickory-smoked meats, steaks, chops, chicken, and seafood. Open Tuesday through Saturday 5 to 8 P.M. Reasonable prices and ample parking. Call 314-443-6212.

The Original Bobby Buford Restaurant. Stadium Building at I-70, next to the Hilton Inn. Three levels are decorated with sunlight and plants. There is an interesting menu with well-planned daily luncheon specials. Open daily from 11:30 A.M. Reasonable prices. Call 314-445-8647.

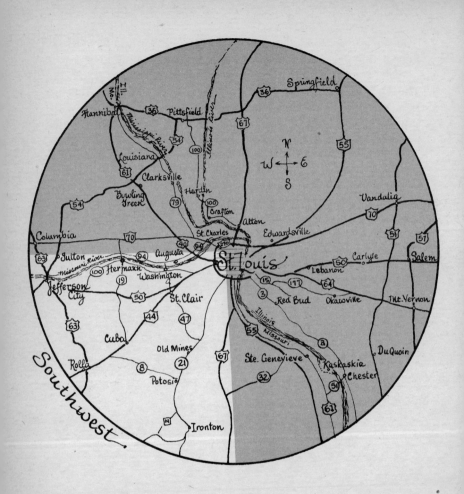

SOUTHWEST

DAY TRIP I

Jefferson City

Westphalia

Bonnots Mill

St. Aubert

Frankenstein

Chamois

Deer

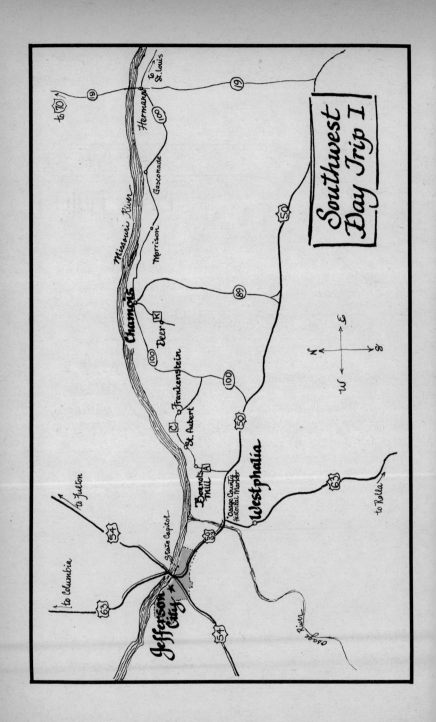

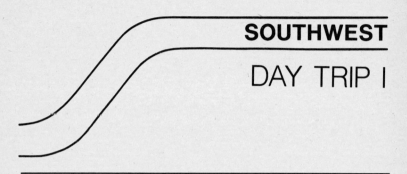

SOUTHWEST

DAY TRIP I

JEFFERSON CITY

It was the German immigrants who brought their culture to this small metropolis located at the intersections of U.S. 54, 63, and 50. At one time city ordinances prohibited the erection of a frame building, and Jefferson City became known as the "Town of Brick." Buildings constructed by early brickmasons and stonemasons still stand today. The town was incorporated in 1825 and the first state capitol building was completed in 1826 on the site of what is now the Governor's Mansion. A fire destroyed the old state capitol and it was replaced, but it too burned in 1911. The present capitol building was constructed in 1924. To reach the capitol area, immediately after crossing the Missouri River on U.S. 54 take the Main Street exit and go left until you come to the following sites.

WHERE TO GO

State Capitol Building. The capitol's grand stairway is said to be one of the widest staircases in the world and a mammoth bronze door is reputed to be among the largest built in this century. Free guided tours are conducted weekdays every half hour from 8 A.M. to 4 P.M. and every hour (on the hour) on weekends. For more information contact the Information Desk in the rotunda. Call 314-751-4127.

The Governor's Mansion. 100 Madison Street. The mansion was constructed in 1871 and has served 29 first families. Few structural changes have been made since it was built. Private living quarters for the resident first family are on the second floor. Public tours of the mansion's main floor are given each Monday and Wednesday at 10 and 11 A.M. and 1 P.M., except during August, December, and on holidays, or when the mansion is in use for official functions. Phone ahead for reservations. Call 314-751-4141.

Cole County Historical Society. 109 Madison Street. The Society maintains a museum in the historic Governor B. Gratz Brown house, which contains items dating from the time Jefferson City was a part of the Louisiana Territory. Of particular interest is the Society's collection of inaugural ball gowns worn by former First Ladies of Missouri. Open Tuesday through Saturday 1 to 5 P.M. Admission fee. Call 314-635-1850.

Jefferson Landing Historic Site. At the foot of Jefferson Street between the capitol and the Governor's Mansion. At one time this busy shipping center on the Missouri River was often lined with steamboats. Now the landing contains three restored buildings, including the Lohman Building, which houses a Visitor's Center open daily 8 A.M. to 4:30 P.M. No admission fee. Call 314-751-3475.

Missouri State Museum. First floor of the capitol building. The History Hall documents Missouri's growth as a state and the Resources Hall features exhibits on Missouri's natural and man-made resources. Open daily 8 A.M. to 5 P.M. No admission fee.

Highway Patrol Museum. 1510 East Elm Street. The museum offers free tours with advance notice Monday through Friday.

A Safety Education Center has recently been added, emphasizing traffic safety. Other exhibits document the 50-year history of the highway patrol. Call 314-751-3313, ext. 115.

WESTPHALIA

As you leave Jefferson City, take U.S. 50 east to M-63 and travel 4 miles (6.4 km) south to Westphalia. This sleepy village was the focal point of a very early German Catholic migration. St. Joseph's Church and School dominate this picturesque town even today, protectively embracing the surrounding countryside and its old-world farmsteads. The Osage County Historical Society maintains a small office and museum near the church.

WHERE TO GO

St. Joseph's Church. Main Street. The stained-glass windows in this beautiful church were a gift from an early priest who had them fabricated in his German homeland and shipped to America. The organ is known throughout the world. It was a gift from an early Westphalia doctor. Be sure to notice the elegant wrought iron hinges gracing the massive doors on all sides of the majestic church. Call 314-455-2320.

WHERE TO EAT

Westphalia Inn. Main Street. The sign in front advises "Gute Deutsche Kost" and you'd expect nothing less than good German cooking in this quaint village. This restaurant has long been known for fried chicken and country ham dinners served family style. Open weekdays 5 to 8 P.M. Sundays noon to 8 P.M. Reasonable prices. Closed January and February. 314-455-9991.

BONNOTS MILL— ST. AUBERT— FRANKENSTEIN

Return to U.S. 50 via U.S. 63 and take a few moments to linger at the Osage County historical marker. Let the tranquility of the countryside envelop you as you continue east on U.S. 50. Turn left at County Road A to three unique and lovely river towns that appear untouched by time. Bonnots Mill is the oldest, dating from the French settlement. Frame homes clinging to the hillsides mirror the early activity of this river town.

The river that brought early industry has left St. Aubert . . . and so have most of the people. Four or five buildings remain, including one brick edifice that once was a hotel serving the railroad and the river. After several years as a general store, it now is a private residence. The nearby ice house that was once filled with river ice for the community struggles to survive.

Frankenstein is located on County Road C. Here the elegant church dominates the countryside and still meets the needs of farm families descended from the early settlers.

This part of Missouri is full of little villages with names like Freedom, Useful, Hope, Crook, Aud, and Welcome. While the majority now are only highway markers, summertime picnics are held in most of them. Beginning in May and continuing through the summer each Sunday there is a community playing host to the public with excellent country food, bazaars, bake sales, and games for young people. If you're in the area, you'll be most welcome.

CHAMOIS

County Road C is a pretty drive all the way to M-100, where you turn left and continue on to the picturesque village of

Chamois. Established in 1818, Chamois was named for the settlers' alpine homeland, where a goatlike antelope frequented
the hillsides. The prehistoric people in this area were Mound
Builders, followed by the Osage, Delaware, and Shawnee Indians. Chamois was a steamboat stop for years and much of the
community's entertainment centered around the riverfront. In
the 1870s, however, Chamois became a railroad hub and a
roundhouse was built, bringing new families and expanded
trade to the area. Chamois has six beautiful churches to serve a
population of 615.

DEER

Just 4 miles (6.4 km) south of Chamois on County Road K is
Deer. At one time it was an important stop on the post road
from Chamois to St. James. The earliest settler is reputed to
have walked to Deer from St. Louis, staked out his land, and
walked back to St. Louis, to return later. The church still marks
the site of this early settlement and twice each year services are
held there. The summer service is also a homecoming picnic in
the tradition of other small communities.

Returning to Chamois and M-100, you are 14 miles (22.5
km) from Hermann, and nearly halfway home to St. Louis.

SOUTHWEST

DAY TRIP II

Hermann
Rhineland
Starkenburg

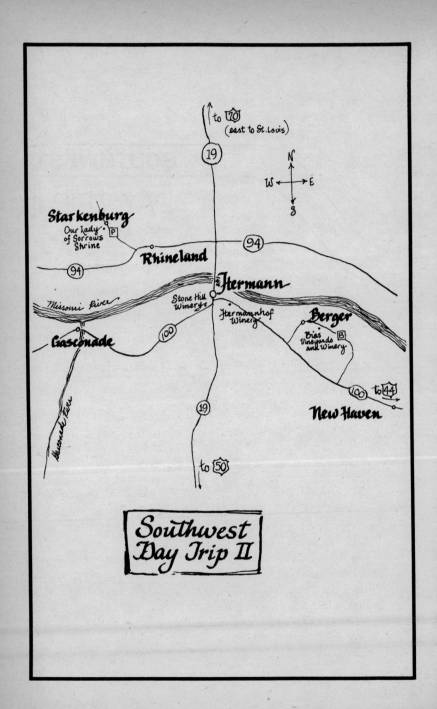

to 70
(east to St. Louis)

19

N
W ← → E
S

Starkenburg
Our Lady
of Sorrows
Shrine
P

Rhineland

94

94

Missouri River

Hermann

Stone Hill
Winery

Hermannhof
Winery

Berger

Bias
Vineyards
and Winery
B

Gasconade

100

Missouri River

100   to 44

19

New Haven

to 50

**Southwest
Day Trip II**

HERMANN

Located at the junction of M-100 and M-19, Hermann was Missouri's best-kept secret until the *New Yorker* magazine called the nation's attention to this timeless picture-book village a few years back. Not much has changed since it was settled in the 1830s by thrifty, industrious German immigrants. The German Settlement Society of Philadelphia selected this particular area to establish a new home. Here they could escape the uninterrupted wars of the fatherland and build a new environment. Fascinated with its old-world charm, newsman Harry Reasoner chose Hermann's cemetery for his CBS evening newscast in 1977. A year later, the West German Broadcasting Company spent a week documenting the everyday life in Hermann.

The town is a bit more modern than it was in the last century. Yet it still adheres to the tenets laid down by the small group of settlers who tenaciously began to carve a town out of the hills, valleys, and creeks in 1837. They named their village Hermann, after a German patriot, and proudly insisted that it have a Market Street 10 feet wider than Philadelphia's! Today the town does, indeed, have a Market Street that meets this requirement.

Pride was also the hallmark of the skilled artisans and tradesmen who came here. Many of the old buildings that stand today mirror their dedication to quality brick masonry, stonecutting, carpentry, and ironworking. Hermann's two historic districts contain more than 100 buildings, uniquely German in design and construction, that are in the National Register of Historic Places.

Along with their building talents, the Germans brought with them a natural ability for winemaking. By 1847, grape growing and wine manufacturing were major industries in the town. At one time, the Stone Hill Wine Company was the third largest winery in the world and the second largest in the United States.

In the early 1900s, Missouri supplied one-twelfth of the wine consumed in America. Much of the wine was from small wineries like those in Hermann. (Hermann is within 50 miles, or 80.5 km, of ten wineries and the major vineyards of Missouri.)

While the town has not grown as large as the early settlers hoped, it still is home to 2,500 persons who are intent on living an unhurried life while the rest of the world rushes by. Hermann attracts tourists from all over the nation who come to take part in the annual celebrations held here from March through December. Some events and places to visit include:

WHERE TO GO

Stone Hill Winery. Stone Hill Highway and Goethe Street. Perched dramatically on a hilltop with the largest series of arched cellars in America buried in its slopes, this facility has been restored and is once again vinting wines. Stone Hill began to make wine in 1847 and by the turn of the century it had become the second largest in the United States, producing over 1 million gallons a year. Today, you can tour the winery and sample the wines. If you like what you taste, you can buy all you want at reasonable prices. Tours and tasting are available all day Monday through Saturday and Sunday afternoons. Don't miss the tower cupola, which affords a breathtaking view of Hermann. To arrange for group tours, contact Stone Hill Winery, Route 1, Box 26, Hermann, MO 65041, or call 314-486-2221. There is a fee for the tour.

There is also the Vintage 1847 Restaurant next door that serves wine and German food. It's open daily 11 A.M. to 10 P.M.

Hermannhof Winery. 330 East First Street. The Hermannhof Winery invites you to take a tour of its underground cellars and to sample their blended and aged American and European wines. The winery is open daily. Admission fee. Call 314-486-5959.

Bias Vineyards and Winery. Take M-100 7 miles (11.3 km) east of Hermann to County Road B and proceed 3½ miles (5.6 km) through Berger while watching for signs to the vineyard. This winery occupies a historic bluff-top farm overlooking lush Missouri River bottomlands. Current wines include a fine dry wine and a sweet table wine. For more information call 314-834-5475.

Deutscheim Historic Site. 109 West Second Street. This site consists of two historic homes: the Pommer-Gentner House (Market Street) and the Strehly House. The Gentner House reflects the Greek revival and Federal architectural influences. The Strehly House was the location of the first printshop in Hermann. A German-language newspaper was published in the basement. A tour includes a look at the attached winery, the residence, and the printshop. Reservations should be made a week in advance. Admission fee. Call 314-486-2200.

German School Museum. 312 Schiller Street. This museum is actually three in one: a children's museum, which includes toys and children's furniture; the River Museum, which memorializes the rivermen who plied the Missouri when navigation was hazardous; and a general museum of artifacts from the Hermann and Gasconade areas. Open daily, April 1 through November 1. Admission fee. Call 314-486-2017.

Antique Mall. 117 East Second Street. Hermann's former Muzik Halle now hosts a collection of quality antique shops within easy walking distance of restaurants, museums, and historic homes. Open daily 9 A.M. to 5 P.M. They will be happy to refer you to other area shops and country auctions. Call 314-486-2148.

Kramer Fresh Fish. At the foot of Schiller Street on the river. Missouri River catfish, dressed and cut, are sold here, as are buffalo fish and carp, or whatever else the day's catch may bring.

Red Barn Craft Shop, Wilding's Gallery, Antiques, and Museum. 523 West Ninth Street. The craft shop offers a bit of everything from work by artists and craftsmen in the Hermann area to a complete line of arts and crafts supplies. Across from this shop is a 100-year-old frame barn that houses Wilding's Gallery. In the loft is a museum of life-sized birds carved by Clem Wilding, one of Missouri's best-known woodcarvers. There is also a large collection of antique tools and equipment used by early settlers. The first floor of the barn is packed with country antiques, old tools, crocks, furniture, and more. Tours daily 10 A.M. to 5:30 P.M.; Sundays 1 to 4 P.M. Admission fee for the Gallery. Call 314-486-5544.

Sausage Shops. On any given day, you can probably buy 30 kinds of sausage in Hermann. To begin with, no sausagemaker seasons his product like any other and that's what makes the difference. There's summer sausage, braunschweiger, German bologna, bratwurst, knackwurst, mettwurst, etc. They are available at these shops: Loutre Food Market, M-19 and M-94; Riverfront Bi-Rite, 225 East First Street; Hermannhof Winery, 330 East First Street; and Jay's IGA, M-19 and Sixth Street.

WHERE TO EAT

The Calico Cupboard. 4 Schiller Street. Bill and Betty Taylor have used early Hermann antiques and turn-of-the-century furnishings to make you feel right at home with their style of traditional German fare. Take your own wine or beer and enjoy a home-cooked meal with bountiful portions. If you're lucky enough to be there when they feature chicken noodle soup, take advantage of it. The noodles are homemade and the soup is rich enough to cure whatever ails you. On weekends there's a Bauernschmaus (farmer's feast) that includes seven meats, seven vegetables, seven salads and desserts. There's a special children's menu for little ones under six years old. The restaurant also offers antiques and crafts items for sale. Moderate prices. Open Monday through Friday 11 A.M. to 2 P.M.; Saturday and Sunday 11 A.M. to 8 P.M. A peasant's breakfast buffet is served weekends 8 to 11 A.M. Reservations are suggested for groups. Call 314-486-2030.

The Concert Hall. 206 First Street. The oldest tavern in continuous operation west of the Mississippi, the Concert Hall was built in 1878. It originally contained a tavern and dining room on the first floor and a concert hall on the second. It also housed Hermann's first two-lane bowling alley and from 1915 to 1923 it was the only motion-picture house in town. It is now open for parties and dances on the second floor. The public may dine at the Concert Hall Bar & Barrel, a pastime that the owner, a former sheriff, will tell you is not at all against the law. Open 6 A.M. to midnight. Call 314-486-9989.

WHERE TO STAY

Der Klingerbaunn Inn. 108 East Second Street (across the street from Deutscheim Historic Site). This three-story Victorian home built in 1878 has been restored and refurbished with antiques reflecting Missouri's heritage. The inn offers bed and breakfast at moderate prices. Open 7 days a week, year round. The place is small and intimate, so be sure to make reservations in advance. 314-486-2030.

SPECIAL EVENTS

A festive atmosphere prevails in Hermann and the countryside beginning with the first blooms of spring on the hillsides through the brilliant colors of the fall foliage. All events commemorate German traditions and the German hero Hermann, who led fellow patriots into battle against the Roman army in A.D. 9. Festival weekends always include crafts, special exhibits, home tours, German music, antique markets, German food, and German wine.

Volksmarsch. In the tradition of the German walkfests, the Volksmarsch is held the third weekend in September and attracts walkers from many states and foreign countries. To participate in this noncompetitive family sport, contact Hermann Volksport Association, Route 1, Hermann, MO. 65041. Call 314-486-2737.

The Wurstfest. First full weekend in March. No pun intended, this is the best Wurst festival in Missouri. Visitors can sample bratwurst, knackwurst, bockwurst, and other sausage specialties that allow Hermann to claim the title of "Sausage Capital of Missouri." Call 314-486-2030.

Maifest. Third weekend in May. This is Hermann's oldest and best-known festival; it attracts thousands of visitors each year. Maifest offers traditional German food and entertainment. Call 314-486-2017.

Great Stone Hill Grape Stomp. Second Saturday in August. This is the day for contestants to roll up their pant legs for an afternoon of fun and games.

Octoberfest. Last three weekends in October. Visitors may sample the fine wines of Stone Hill Winery as they soak in the lovely autumn color from the hillside. Call 314-486-2221.

RHINELAND

If you want to take a couple of little side trips before heading back to St. Louis, you might drive across the Missouri River on M-19 to M-94 and follow it west as it winds its way through Rhineland, a picturesque German village that thrives on agriculture.

Rhineland's famed Wurstjaeger Dancers have spread the traditional German love of music and dancing throughout the United States and Europe. Originally, the Wurstjaegers were part of a pre-Lenten celebration that ended with a masked ball the night before Lent. Over the years the masks have given way to colorful costumes and authentic German dancing. Arrangements for the dancers to appear at any event may be made by calling 314-236-4398.

STARKENBURG

A mile (1.6 km) west of Rhineland, take a right from M-94 to County Road P north to Starkenburg. You'll pass through 3 magnificent miles (4.8 km) of countryside similar to that of the Rhine Valley in Germany before arriving at the lovely shrine to Our Lady of Sorrows. Built of native stone quarried in the nearby hills, the shrine reflects the gratitude felt by early priests and parishioners who found a secure home in the new world. Each spring and fall the shrine hosts a pilgrimage that attracts many visitors. The location of this beautiful chapel overlooking the mist-shrouded hills and meadows encourages one to pause for thought. The grounds and grottoes, the paths for quiet walks through the natural wooded setting, all rekindle the faith felt by these early settlers. Starkenburg will soon be added to the National Register of Historic Places. Open year round, weather permitting.

SOUTHWEST

DAY TRIP III

Gasconade County
Gasconade City
Fredericksburg
First Creek

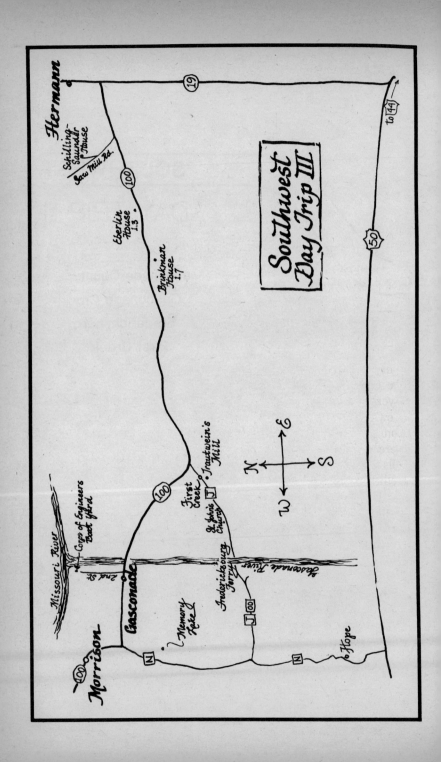

Southwest
Day Trip III

SOUTHWEST
DAY TRIP III

GASCONADE COUNTY

Every type of topography imaginable can be found in Gasconade County, from rolling hills in the north near the Missouri River to lush valleys and open farmland in the south. Gasconade County was created from broken Ozark plateau worn down from ancient mountain heights and bluffs bared by erosion. Here you'll find active waterways, pastures shaded by wooded hills with an abundance of redbud, dogwood, and wildflowers. In the autumn, the flaming foliage is a seasonal celebration.

Early settlers along Frene Creek found a ready food supply in the valley's abundant wildlife. Today Gasconade County lures hundreds of hunters during the deer and turkey seasons. For five years Gasconade County has reported the largest deer kill in the state, and its turkey harvest ranks in the top ten counties.

M-100 crosses the county east and west and M-19 traverses it from north to south. As you leave M-19 at Hermann, you head west on M-100 through some of the oldest settled valleys in Missouri.

The drive will take you past small farms identified by the

47

clusters of well-maintained buildings and green pastures. The limestone that attracted the German immigrants to this area is evident in the stone buildings and homes along the way. They stand, a century later, as Gibraltar-like monuments to the skill and foresight of the builders. Some of these stone structures include:

WHERE TO GO

The Schilling-Saunders Home. Near Hermann, ¾ mile (1.2 km) west of M-19 at Sawmill Road and 1 mile (1.6 km) north on the right (see map). This home was built in the 1840s to support extensive vineyards and winemaking by the Schilling family. Now used as the weekend retreat of the Saunders family, the home boasts a wonderful full-length porch reminiscent of the French period that made porches a vital part of the home. Available for group tours. Call 314-486-2030.

The Brinkman House. Follow M-100 west 1½ miles (2.4 km), past the old Eberlin Home (which sits slantwise with the highway) to the Brinkman home, built in 1855. It is now owned by fifth-generation descendants of the original builders. The mound to your left across Frene Creek is said to be a remnant of an early Indian village.

GASCONADE CITY

The first major road leaving M-100 is County Road J. You may want to take a side trip at this intersection to the site of Trautwein's Mill, fed by the waters of First Creek. It's a pretty place to stop and ponder. During the Civil War, soldiers stopped here and confiscated the flour and meal and used the huge cottonwood stumps for dining tables.

At County Road J, M-100 turns north and continues west

toward Gasconade City and the Gasconade River. Isaac Best
established a mill on the Gasconade River in the 1800s and the
location later became Gasconade City. It was the first county
seat of the original Gasconade County and was nearly the capital of Missouri (it missed out by two votes).

Daniel Boone lived here at one time and was a member of
the first Gasconade County Court. The town is now a popular
fishing village, with public fishing access from the west bank of
the river at the foot of Oak Street, 1 block from M-100. Gasconade Park on the south side of M-100 at First Street offers picnic
areas and rest rooms.

Two blocks from the Gasconade River bridge, Second
Street turns right across the railroad and into the headquarters
of the U.S. Corps of Engineers and the Government Boat Yards.
Open weekdays 7:30 A.M. to 4 P.M. Guide available.

From Gasconade, M-100 continues through beautiful countryside, overlooking peaceful valleys, toward Morrison, a small
village resting quietly at the river's edge. Turn left on County
Road N at the edge of Morrison and continue south overlooking
the Gasconade's valley.

One-half mile (.8 km) down the road is the entrance to
Memory Lake, where you can fish, camp, boat, and picnic.
There is also a snack bar. Open all year, weather permitting.
Modest fee. Call 314-294-3627.

FREDERICKSBURG

Continue south on County Road N to County Road J and east to
Fredericksburg. This burg used to be a busy loading point on
the Gasconade River, where livestock and grain were transported to Hermann for shipment to city markets.

The Fredericksburg ferry across the gentle Gasconade River is the best tourist bargain in Missouri. For a modest fee, your
car and family are transported across the river. As you gaze
across the river at the bluff you've just left, you may marvel at

how these crossings were accomplished in the early years. Occasionally a German-born operator will be on hand to add authenticity to this page from the past.

St. John's Church. Back on dry land again, continue east on County Road J past St. John's Church, a beautiful stone chapel set among the trees and still actively serving the community after 126 years. In 1978, the West German Broadcasting Company selected this congregation and church as the subject of a film on Missouri's German heritage. The churchyard and the songbirds added a quiet benediction to the documentary.

FIRST CREEK

County Road J continues northeasterly through some of the most interesting parts of the countryside, geologically, before it reaches the valley of First Creek, ½ mile (.8 km) south of M-100. The trading post here was known as Gaebler. Across the road, Bruen's Grove was a popular site for picnics and tent shows. A half mile (.8 km) north, County Road J intersects M-100. The drive back to Hermann provides equally interesting views and insight into the skill and cunning of those first settlers who called this valley home.

SOUTHWEST

DAY TRIP IV

August A. Busch
Memorial Wildlife Area
Weldon Spring
Wildlife Area
Howell Island Access
Daniel Boone's Home
Defiance
Matson
Augusta
Femme Osage
Dutzow
Luxenhaus
Washington
Gray Summit

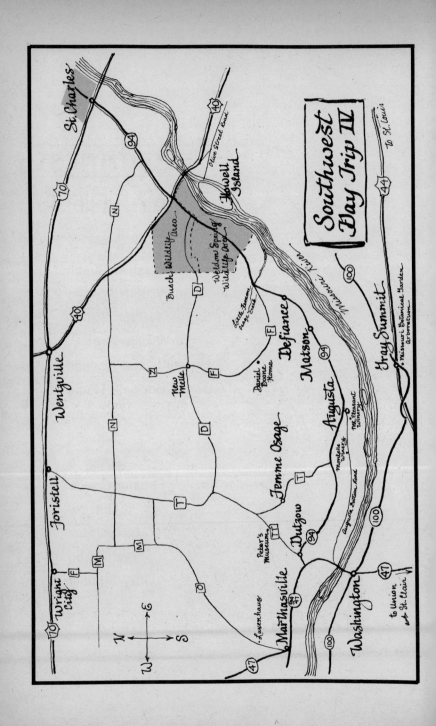

Southwest
Day Trip IV

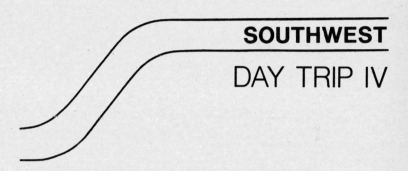

SOUTHWEST
DAY TRIP IV

Nestled in the purple blue haze that shrouds the hills is Missouri's Rhine Country—a place where Germans weary of civil war in their country found peace and promise of an environment where they could raise their families. The countryside, with its beautiful hills and valleys, so resembled their own that they settled here to pursue their trades. Their love for beauty is seen in each well-laid stone structure, each arched doorway, every stone lintel and doorstep, and in the handwrought hinges and brackets.

To experience the Rhine country, you leave I-70 at M-94 and head southwest from St. Charles. From here you'll wend your way through the following places of interest:

AUGUST A. BUSCH MEMORIAL WILDLIFE AREA— WELDON SPRING WILDLIFE AREA— HOWELL ISLAND ACCESS

As M-94 crosses M-40 and M-61, you'll enter this wildlife area that covers 7,000 acres and includes 32 lakes used as resting areas for waterfowl and hardy winter birds. Thousands of migrating songbirds and Canada geese migrate here each year. You will also see the scattered remains of 100 ammunition storage bunkers constructed during World War II. The area is open 6 A.M. to 10 P.M. Fishing and hunting fees. Call 314-623-4688.

Across the way on the east side of M-94 is the Weldon Spring Wildlife Area containing 7,200 acres. It is open 5 A.M. to 10 P.M.

To reach Howell Island Access, take M-40 across the Missouri River and take the first right (Chesterfield Airport Road). Make another right to Olive Street Road and drive 1 mile (1.6 km) to a sign that says Howell Island. It offers 2,500 acres to roam in and is open 5 A.M. to 10 P.M. Call 314-623-4688.

Daniel Boone's Home

M-94 continues south through a wonderful landscape with beautiful vistas on either side. Cross Little Femme Osage Creek and take County Road F west to Daniel Boone's home. This region is a mix of well-kept working farms and restored early Missouri homes. It's quiet here and, if you pause for a minute, you just might spot a coyote bounding through the fields.

Boone's home is a Georgian structure, built between 1803 and 1810. Inside there are mantels and woodwork carved by Boone from Missouri walnut. The beautifully kept grounds include the "Judgment Tree" under which Boone is said to have held court. The home is open March 15 to December 15 9:30 A.M. to dusk; December 15 to March 15, it is open weekends only. There are camping facilities nearby and a museum and gift shop on the grounds. For information and group tour rates call 314-987-2221.

DEFIANCE

Head south on M-94 to Defiance, a town with an interesting

history. Before the Civil War, Defiance was called Darst Bottoms. Its citizens, envious of other communities along the newly built railroad, built a depot to lure the railroad away from other Missouri towns such as Augusta. They aptly renamed the town Defiance and built a unique frame church high on a hill to add a touch of simple, eloquent beauty.

MATSON

Driving southwest on M-94 you'll pass acres of Missouri River bottomland and farms spread out toward the river. In the distance are towering limestone bluffs, washed white by the ages. All this is a prelude to Matson.

If there had been a Boone, Missouri, it should have been located here. Daniel Boone actually received a grant from the Spanish government in exchange for bringing settlers to "Upper Louisiana."

Leaving Matson, you'll see a mountain of rock to your left known as "Berg's Crossing," a place that provides building stone for present-day construction. The ascent affords a beautiful view of the Missouri River on the left, and a breathtaking panorama of "old-world" countryside on the right. In the distance, you'll see Augusta as you head south on M-94.

AUGUSTA

You'll reach Augusta heading southwest on M-94. The southern slopes and fertile soil of this area were recognized by the wine-conscious Germans back in 1836 as a spot appropriate for vineyards. Named after their native Augusta, Germany, the townspeople had built 11 wineries by 1850.

During the riverboat years, Augusta was a favorite destination for St. Louis honeymooners, and would probably be a large city today if it hadn't been for the flood of 1872 that changed the river's course, leaving it 12 miles (19.3 km) from the nearest shipping point! However, the wineries continued to thrive and in 1980 Augusta became the first designated wine district in the United States, which means that these regional wines have special characteristics that reflect the soil and climate.

Augusta is a walkabout town with many interesting shops, all within short distance of one another. The thoroughfares are well marked and easily reached on foot. Some fun visits include:

WHERE TO GO

Augusta Wood Shop. Features custom-made furniture, toys, Shaker racks and gifts. Call 314-228-4406.

Copper Star Gallery. Michael Anton Bruckdorfer's love of nature is reflected in his craft. Glassblowing will take on a new dimension after a visit with Michael. Call 314-228-4494.

Mt. Pleasant Winery. Flanked by producing vineyards, this winery's dry European-type wines have brought it many awards. Tours of the cellars, winery, and vineyards are free with the purchase of wine. Open weekdays 10 A.M. to 5:30 P.M.; Sunday noon to 5:30 P.M.

Eve's Cheese Wedge. Adjacent to the Mt. Pleasant Winery. You can select an aged cheese to accompany your wine and relax on Mt. Pleasant's inviting terrace to ponder the intricacies of the wine-making process and the beauty of the quaint village. Call 314-228-4419.

Montelle Winery and Vineyards. Reached via M-94 or the Augusta Bottom Road alongside the winery. Set in the woods, the winery is about 2½ miles (4 km) south of Augusta. It offers a variety of good hybrid wines. Open year round, weekdays 10 A.M. to 6 A.M.; Sunday 1 to 6 P.M. Call 314-228-4464.

WHERE TO EAT

Ivy Dene's Sourdough Bakery. The fragrance of fresh-baked breads will draw you here like a magnet. Breads are baked fresh daily from natural ingredients. Open Tuesday through Sunday 9 A.M. to 5 P.M.

Lee La Point's Farmer's Hotel. This spot invites you to bring a hearty appetite. Simple, but beautifully decorated, the surroundings allow you to focus on Lee's excellent food. Daily entrees are most satisfying and are sprinkled with herbs from her own garden. There are also luscious soups, sandwiches, and excellent desserts. Seating is limited and prices reasonable (dinner from $9). Check on availability of seating as you walk about the town, then look forward with great anticipation to a fine meal. Call 314-228-4410.

FEMME OSAGE

From Augusta, head north on County Road T to Femme Osage, a picture-book village of early Missouri. The glistening white frame church and old stone schoolhouse are charming reminders of a world that you might have thought gone forever. Take a camera and try to arrive in the late afternoon for the best pictures. The Femme Osage Antique Shop hosts all of the buildings open to the public and it is open Wednesday through Sunday 11 A.M. to 5 P.M. Don't miss the Mad Hatters Ice Cream Party, an ice-cream shop decorated with old millinery items. Call 314-228-4821.

DUTZOW

To reach Dutzow you can travel one of two ways: continue north on County Road T from Femme Osage until you reach the intersection of County Road TT and double back south; or go back to Augusta and leave via M-94. You'll wend your way to Dutzow, an old but well-scrubbed German settlement that is still an active trading center. Some 2½ miles (4 km) north of Dutzow is *Peters Stone Age Museum* offering a collection of Indian artifacts and early Missouri primitives. Admission fee. Call 314-433-2683 for an appointment.

LUXENHAUS

Luxenhaus is a collection of log buildings from all around Missouri, preserved and assembled in a setting that documents the building skill of early settlers. To reach it, continue west on M-94 to Marthasville. Turn right on M-47 and drive north 2½ miles (4 km) to County Road O and Luxenhaus.

The setting here includes a covered bridge in the Eric Sloane tradition, a forge barn, smokehouse, and antiques shop. Owned and occupied by the Hostketter family, Luxenhaus is open Wednesday through Friday. An appointment is necessary. Admission fee. Call 314-433-5669.

WASHINGTON

To end your Day Trip, travel south from Luxenhaus on County Road O until you hit M-47. Head south across the river to Washington, a peaceful little town that was laid out on the banks of the Missouri in 1839. It is famous for two rather unusual things: its former zither factory and its corncob pipes. High-quality zithers, so much a part of the German musical tradition, were produced during Washington's early years. Corncob pipe manufacture was also established in the early 1800s. Today there are two factories in Washington—Missouri Meerschaum Company (which supplied pipes for General Douglas Mac-Arthur) and Buescher's Cob Pipes. Together these companies make Washington the "Corncob Pipe Capital of the World." If you see corncob pipes being smoked in France, Africa, or England, you can bet they came from Missouri.

Tours of the Buescher factory are conducted at their St. Clair branch (see I-44 tour) but may be arranged by calling 314-239-4792.

WHERE TO EAT

Elijah McClean's. 600 West Front Street in Washington. This delightful dining room is set in the former home of a Washington doctor. The spacious grounds overlook the river, and the domed ceilings and massive woodwork throughout prepare you for the unhurried world of the past, with excellent dining and attentive service. A variety of entrees is served at reasonable prices. Travel back to St. Louis, pausing along M-100 at Gray Summit. Call 314-239-4404. Reservations recommended.

GRAY SUMMIT

From Washington, you can travel east on M-100 and the intersection of I-44 to Gray Summit. Here you'll find more than 2,000 acres of meandering trails and wildflowers that make up the Missouri Botanical Garden Arboretum. Groves of trees, including redbud and dogwood, line the road on either side. The Pinetum is a collection of pine trees from around the world. Their majestic greenery is mirrored in Pinetum lake. You can hike for 10 miles (16.1 km) on trails through oak, hickory, and maple forests and admire the view of the Meramac River valley from atop the limestone bluffs. Open daily 8 A.M. to 5 P.M. Admission fee. Call 314-577-5138.

SOUTHWEST

DAY TRIP V

Lone Elk Park

Six Flags over Mid-America

St. Clair

Meramec Caverns (Stanton)

Onondaga Cave (Leasburg)

Wine and Grape Country

St. James

Rolla, Doolittle, and Newburg

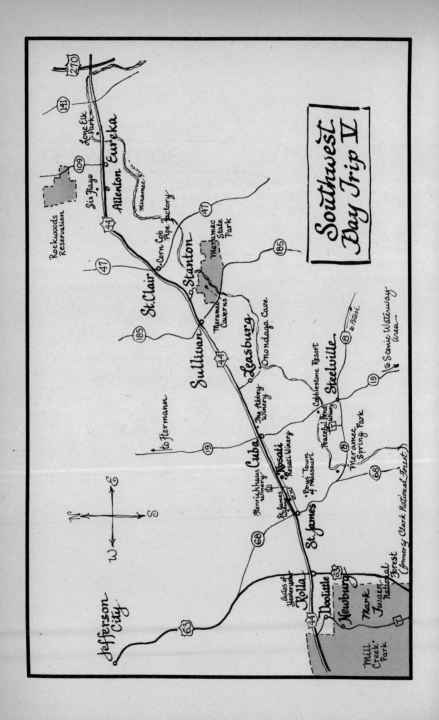

Southwest
Day Trip V

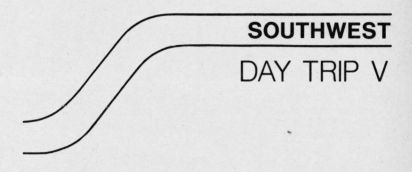

LONE ELK PARK

This is a prelude to the wonderful trip ahead. Situated at the intersection of I-44 and M-141, Lone Elk Park can be your first stop on the journey south. Spread over 400 acres, the park is a refuge for elk, white-tailed deer, Barbados sheep, great horned owls, Canada geese, mallards, and other waterfowl. Open daily 8 A.M. to dusk. No camping. No admission fee.

SIX FLAGS OVER MID-AMERICA

Just 15 miles (24.1 km) from I-270 and I-44, the Allenton exit takes you to a fairytale adventure. If you exit north to Melrose Road and east to Glencoe Road, you can travel to Rockwoods Reservation, a wildlife refuge operated by the Missouri Conservation Commission. It's a haven for many wild birds and animals.

If you venture south, you'll find excitement at Six Flags

Over Mid-America, a 200-acre theme park that offers 100 different rides, shows, and attractions, plus big-name entertainment. A one-day ticket includes everything but food and drink. (To save money, you can take a picnic lunch.) Open May 20 to September 1, 10 A.M. to 10 P.M. Group rates available. Call 1-800-325-3187 or 1-800-392-3727.

ST. CLAIR

Take M-47 exit at St. Clair left to Commercial Street, ½ mile (.8 km). Turn right on Commercial Street to Buescher's Cob Pipes Factory, which offers free self-conducted tours for groups or individuals. Tours can be taken Monday through Thursday 7:30 A.M. to 3 P.M. (except at noon). For more information, call 314-239-4792 or write P.O. Box 265, Washington, MO 63090.

MERAMEC CAVERNS (STANTON)

One of Missouri's most interesting assets is its caves. In fact, Missouri is known as "the cave state," with over 4,000 caves, and more being discovered each year. The Meramec River valley provides one of the most lovely natural areas in the region as well as a good portion of the state's caves. Only a few are open to visitors; for instance, the Meramec Caverns, discovered in 1716 and used at that time for shelter and storage. In 1760, Spanish miners used the cave for lead mining operations. Gun powder was produced and stored in the cave during the Civil War and the caverns also became a refuge for fugitives on the Underground Railway. The James brothers, along with Frank Dalton and the Younger brothers, used the cave frequently during the 1870s as a hideout.

To reach Meramec Caverns take the Stanton exit south to La Jolla Natural Park. Well-trained tour guides will take you through the caverns on well-lighted walkways. Take along a jacket to protect yourself from the natural air-conditioning (60° F, 16° C). And, take your camera to catch a picture of a stalagmite or two. Open 8 A.M. to dusk in summer and 8:30 P.M. to dusk in winter. Admission fee.

ONONDAGA CAVE (LEASBURG)

This cave, just south of I-44 at the Leasburg exit, is said to be the largest "living" cave in America. It was discovered by Daniel Boone during his visits to Missouri and at least one version of *Tom Sawyer* was filmed here. Over the years some parts of the cave have been sealed to provide water power. The cave was reopened to tourists in time for the St. Louis World's Fair in 1904. A network of safe lighted walkways permits visitors to walk through the cave, now owned and operated by the Missouri Park Department. Nearby picnic areas and campgrounds are available along with boating and fishing.

WINE AND GRAPE COUNTRY

From the wooded cave area, the countryside blends into rolling hills especially suited for grape culture. Vineyards and winemaking were a major part of Missouri's past and are now a significant part of the state's future. More than 20 varieties of wine are being produced here, ranging from sweet Concords to dry French hybrids and vinifera types. Missouri's resurgent wine industry has resulted in Augusta, Missouri, becoming the first designated winemaking district in the United States. (See p. 55).

The Abbey. Take the Cuba exit from I-44 to this newly established winery. You'll see it alongside the highway as you approach the exit. Opened in 1980 by Lucian Dressel, an Augusta vintner, it features wine made from locally grown grapes. Open daily. Call 314-885-2168.

Peaceful Bend Vineyard and Winery. Just 12 miles (19.3 km) south of M-19 at the Cuba exit is Steelville and M-8. Turn right on M-8 and right again at County Road T. Continue 2 miles (3.2 km) to the winery owned by Dr. A. N. Arneson. His three wines are named for the nearby rivers of Meramec, Courtois, and Huzzah. He uses only his own estate-grown grapes. Call 314-775-2578.

Cobblestone Resort. As you return to Cuba via M-19, this resort is on your left 2 miles (3.2 km) north of Steelville. It offers family lodging, food, and recreation during the summer, from May 15 to October 1. Situated on the Meramec River, the resort provides canoe trips, fishing, and other family sports. Call 314-775-2939.

ST. JAMES

Back on I-44 at Cuba, continue west to St. James, known as the "Forest City of the Ozarks." It is also the home of three wineries and extensive grape-growing operations that early Italian settlers established on their arrival here. St. James is also the home of Boys Town of Missouri, Missouri Veterans' Home, and Meramec Spring Park. Nearby, the Woods Memorial Area attracts wildlife enthusiasts.

Rosati Winery. Right outside St. James, this winery is the oldest in the area, having been established by early Italian immigrants. During Prohibition, wine grapes were sold to Welch Grape Juice processors. Seventeen wines may be sampled at

the end of your tour here. Open year round, daily 9 A.M. to 6
P.M.; Sundays noon to 6 P.M. Call 314-265-8629.

Ashby's. At St. James exit take the south outer road (ZZ) and
follow the signs to County Road KK. At Ashby's, oak aging
casks and four concrete fermentation tanks (named for apostles)
speak of bygone years. This is Concord grape country, but
Ashby's wines range from sweet to dry. There is an extensive
apple orchard on the premises, so a fall visit is doubly reward-
ing. Open year round, daily 8 A.M. to 6 P.M. Groups should call
in advance. Call 314-265-8629.

Heinrichhaus Winery. Continue on County Road KK east of
County Road U overpass and turn left (north) to the winery
owned by Heinrich Grohe. A native of the Rhine Valley in Germany, he produces light, dry table wines in the European tradition. He also sells fresh grapes in season. During the summer,
crafts and pottery are sold here. Take a picnic lunch and enjoy
the wine of your choice. Open daily 10 A.M. to 6 P.M.; Sunday
noon to 6 P.M. Weekends only after Labor Day. Call 314-265-
5000.

St. James Winery. Return to St. James via County Road KK and
take the I-44 overpass at St. James to the north service road and the
winery owned by Jim and Pat Hofherr. Twenty different kinds of
wine are produced here including Sweet Concord, Catawba, and
berry wines. They also manufacture a variety of dry wines, cham-
pagne, and mead, which is made from honey. You can take a free,
self-guided tour of the winery year round, daily 8 A.M. to 6 P.M.;
Sundays noon to 6 P.M. Call 314-265-7912.

Meramec Spring Park. From St. James Winery, return to M-68
and head 6 miles (9.7 km) south to this first Registered Natural
Landmark of Missouri. It provides trout fishing from dawn to
dark, March 1 to October 31 for a modest fee. A museum traces
the origin of the Meramec Iron Works and the life of the Shawnee Indians in the area. There are playgrounds, picnic areas,
and walking trails. Call 314-265-2527.

ROLLA, DOOLITTLE, AND NEWBURG

Going west on I-44, you reach Rolla in 7 miles (11.3 km). Take the second Rolla exit (U.S. 63 north) 1 block to the Autos of Yesteryear, a museum of automobiles from 1907 to 1937. Open weekdays only. Admission fee.

Continuing west on I-44, take the Newburg-Doolittle exit 4 miles (6.4 km) beyond Rolla and turn left on County Road T through Doolittle and go 1 mile (1.6 km) farther to Newburg.

Winding left on County Road T takes you through this hillside village to the railroad tracks. In 1880, the Frisco Railroad moved its division point to Newburg. The Roundhouse and the Railroad Hotel Eating House were both opened in 1883 and the town became a tent city of early railroad builders.

County Road T, out of Newburg, leads you across the tracks to Clark National Forest and Mill Creek Park, which offer camping, hiking, and fishing. You may then want to head home or continue on to Jefferson City.

SOUTHWEST

DAY TRIP VI

Hillsboro

Washington State Park

Old Mines

Potosi

Pilot Knob

Ironton

Arcadia

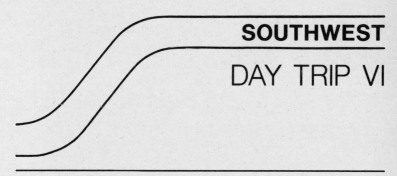

SOUTHWEST
DAY TRIP VI

HILLSBORO

If you take M-21 south of St. Louis, it will lead you straight to the heart of Missouri's mining district and some of the state's most fascinating geologic formations—elephant rocks, mountain peaks, and legendary waterfalls.

One of the first towns you pass through on your trip is Hillsboro, which became a town on February 9, 1839, when it replaced Herculaneum as the Jefferson county seat.

Hugh O'Neal and Samuel Merry donated the land, which sits alongside M-21 about 40 miles (64.4 km) south of St. Louis. Initially, the town was called "Monticello," after Thomas Jefferson's estate. But when the townspeople discovered that another county had already chosen that name for its county seat, it became Hillsboro.

You'll come upon the town quickly after passing Jefferson College, the 400-acre educational center of Jefferson County that sits on a hill just 2 miles (3.2 km) north of Hillsboro. The town may seem small, but it has plenty to offer tourists.

WHERE TO GO

Thomas C. Fletcher Home. Elm and Second streets. Maintained by the Jefferson County Park Department. In 1851, the first native Missourian to serve as governor built this one-and-a-half-story log house. Concerned citizens saved the building from being razed and are now raising money to furnish it. No admission fee. Open by appointment only. Call 314-789-3911.

Hillsboro Horse Show Grounds. Located on M-21 on the outskirts of town. Horse lovers and cowboys should saddle up and head out to the show grounds for two special annual events:

Hillsboro Horse Show and Festival. Sponsored by the Hillsboro Community Civic Club. Each year, horse owners flock to the show grounds to compete in this five-day event held at the end of July and beginning of August. During the show, the family can enjoy the carnival rides, crafts booths, food, and beer tent. Call 314-789-2600.

Jefferson County Championship Rodeo. Sponsored by the Twin City Area Chamber of Commerce. Top-dollar prize money draws some of the country's best cowboys to ride and rope their way through this annual event—held in mid-June. Live entertainment is part of this western roundup that is held at the show grounds. Call 314-937-7697.

Sandy Creek Covered Bridge. 5 miles (8 km) north of Hillsboro on U.S. 21 and 500 feet east of Goldman Road which is also Old Lemay Ferry Road. This bridge is a reminder of Missouri's early transportation system. The 76-foot white pine structure is one of only four covered bridges still standing in the state. Built in 1872 and rebuilt in 1887 and 1940, the bridge still carries traffic.

WHERE TO EAT

Hillsboro Restaurant. Locust and Second streets on the Courthouse Square. The fact that the cafe has been there for around 50 years should tell you something good. You can stop in for a hearty breakfast of bacon and eggs, hash browns, and toast for just over $2. For lunch, try the daily special, which could be anything from corned beef to barbecue. Open Monday through Saturday 7 A.M. to 3 P.M. Closed Sunday. Call 314-789-2216.

WASHINGTON STATE PARK

M-21 south takes you past some of the state's most interesting parks, including this one. Around 20 miles (32.2 km) southwest of Hillsboro and 14 miles (22.5 km) northeast of Potosi, this 1,415-acre park offers a variety of activities.

You can explore the rugged Ozark terrain on the park's three trails. Towering cliffs give a beautiful vista of the southeast Missouri forestlands. A nature center near the entrance explains the park's environment. The Big River, a tributary of the Meramec River, forms the northern boundary. You can fish for bass, bluegill, and catfish or arrange a canoe trip. A swimming pool is open from Memorial Day to Labor Day.

Two sites contain hundreds of rock carvings called petroglyphs, which were carved by prehistoric Indians who used the area as a ceremonial ground between 1000 A.D. and 1600 A.D. The designs range from birds to turkey tracks. Markers explain the importance and meanings of the various symbols.

Camping and picnicking are available year-round, but the regular season is from April 15 to October 31, when water and other sanitary facilities are available. Camping at the tent or trailer sites, including some with electric hook-ups, is available on a first-come first-served basis. No reservations.

If you prefer, one- or two-bedroom cabins may be rented during the regular season. These come with kitchens and air conditioning. For reservations, call 314-586-2995. The same phone numbers can be used to rent canoes and plan two, three, or half-day float trips.

WHERE TO EAT

Thunderbird Dining Lodge. Washington State Park. For convenience and the scenery of the Big River, stop at the stone dining lodge for breakfast, lunch, or dinner. A variety of meals is served at inexpensive prices. Open daily 9 A.M. to 8 P.M. from April 15 to October 31. Call 314-586-6696.

OLD MINES

Heading south on M-21, you'll reach one of the oldest settled areas in the Midwest. The town of Old Mines earned its name from its early link to the lead and barite mining industry. Back in 1723, Philippe Françoise Renault received a land grant from the French government to work a lead mine on a branch of the Meramec River west of the present village.

WHERE TO GO

St. Joachim's Catholic Church. On M-21 just inside the town border. It has been a vital part of the community since its first days. According to legend, three log churches preceded the historic 1828 brick church now standing. Simple, but beautiful, its design is closely related to other Roman Catholic churches built around the same time at Perryville and Ste. Genevieve. Services are held Monday through Saturday at 8:30 A.M., Saturday evening at 5 P.M., and Sundays at 7, 9, and 11 A.M.

POTOSI

South of Old Mines on M-21 is Potosi. Like so many of the

area's towns, the mining industry was responsible for Potosi's growth. Potosi's most famous resident was Moses Austin, whose son, Stephen Fuller Austin, is known as the "Father of Texas." Moses Austin obtained a grant to mine the lead deposits discovered in Potosi in 1773. He later became one of the state's leading industrialists by building the first furnace west of the Allegheny Mountains. He also built a plant for making sheet lead and revolutionized the area's mining industry.

Austin donated 40 acres for a county seat in 1813. Today the town is still linked with the mining industry. Barite and lead are still produced here. In fact, more barite has been mined in this Washington County town than anywhere else in the world! However, the county now ranks third—behind Nevada and Arkansas—in annual production of this mineral.

WHERE TO GO

Moses Austin Grave. Breton Street. In the Presbyterian cemetery, 1 block northwest of the courthouse, a plain boxlike monument marks the grave of Moses Austin. When a depression and the collapse of the Bank of St. Louis in 1818 bankrupted him, Austin discussed the idea of forming a colony in Texas with his son, Stephen, who later carried out their plans. In 1820 Moses Austin rode to San Antonio and settled 300 American colonists. The return journey on horseback ruined his health and he died near Potosi on June 10, 1821.

WHERE TO EAT

Ken's Dine-In. M-21 at the junction of M-8 in the Parkway Shopping Center. The low-priced daily specials here include burgers and chicken. Open Monday through Saturday 10 A.M. to 10 P.M.; Sunday noon to 7 P.M. Call 314-438-2474.

Kennon Cafe. 117 East High Street. If you aren't in a hurry, stop in for some homemade biscuits and gravy, strip steak, or fried clams. The food is sure to please your tastebuds and the price won't hurt your budget. Open Monday through Saturday 6 A.M. to 8 P.M.; Sunday 7 A.M. to 7 P.M. Call 314-438-4921.

PILOT KNOB/IRONTON/ ARCADIA

In the late Dr. Thomas Beveridge's book *Geologic Wonders and Curiosities of Missouri,* these words are found: "An outsider attempting to describe the many unusual and scenic geologic features of the Ironton–Arcadia Valley area feels frustrated in realizing that he could do the area justice only were he to live there for many months and explore the mountains, shut-ins, and many other features on foot."

Beveridge served as Missouri State geologist from 1955 to 1964 and also witnessed the discovery and development of the Viburnum Trend in Iron County, the world's most productive lead-mining district. Discover this area yourself by traveling south down M-21 to the following places:

Pilot Knob

At one time the hill for which the town is named was believed to be composed of solid iron, much like one in the nearby town of Iron Mountain. The world's longest plank road, 12 feet wide and 42 miles (67.6 km) long, connected Iron Mountain and Ste. Genevieve. Ore from Pilot Knob and Iron Mountain was carried over this road by oxcart until the St. Louis and Iron Mountain Railroad was completed in May of 1858. Mining declined when the deposits were discovered to be shallow surface layers.

Before the decline in iron production, Pilot Knob served as a strategic mineral area, particularly during the Civil War. Remnants of one of the state's most bloody battles remain in Pilot Knob.

WHERE TO GO

Fort Davidson State Historic Site. Turn east off M-21 onto County Road V about ¼ mile (.4 km). An iron marker pinpoints the site of the earthen fort built by Union forces to protect the Iron Mountain and Pilot Knob mineral deposits. During September 1864, Confederate Gen. Sterling Price, a native Missourian, was planning a drive toward St. Louis through southeastern Missouri. With a force estimated at 9,000, Price decided to take Fort Davidson to avoid any threat of a flank attack by Union forces. The attack against Gen. Thomas Ewing and his 1,000 Union soldiers began about 2 P.M. on September 27, 1864, and within 20 minutes, 1,200 men (mostly Confederate) were wounded or killed.

Elephant Rocks State Park. Take County Road RA, which doubles back off M-21 about ½ mile (.8 km) to the park entrance. The park actually lies 4 miles (6.4 km) north of Pilot Knob on the north side of Graniteville.

Here, gigantic pink granite boulders stand end to end like elephants at a circus. The boulders were formed more than a billion years ago when molten rock from beneath the earth's surface erupted and then cooled. The granddaddy of Elephant Rocks is aptly named Dumbo. This monolith weighs 680 tons and is 27 feet tall, 35 feet long, and 17 feet wide. The photographers' favorite is Balancing Rock, which sits precariously on the granite ridge.

The park also features the state's first Braille Trail, designated as a National Recreational Trail. It is also wide enough for wheelchairs.

Granite from this area can be found in several historic structures such as the Eads Bridge in St. Louis and the Governor's Mansion in Jefferson City.

There are no campsites, but picnic facilities are available. Fishing is permitted at the park's lake. Call 314-697-5395.

Johnson's Shut-Ins State Park. This 2,386-acre park can be reached by turning west on County Road N off M-21. Take N for about 12½ miles (20.1 km) to the park entrance. One of the most popular state parks, the shut-ins were formed over eons of time as the waters of the Black River cut through a shelf of the oldest exposed rock in Missouri, creating natural water slides for waders and deep pools for adventurous swimmers.

There are 26 campsites and entry is limited to a maximum of 200 vehicles at a time. If you plan to go fishing or swimming here in the summer, you should arrive early. Gates open at 7 A.M. Camping is on a first-come first-served basis. Call 314-546-2450.

WHERE TO EAT

Fort Davidson Cafe. On County Road V in Pilot Knob. This charming spot sits directly across from its namesake. Home-cooked meals have been served here for 30 years. Each day's special—from chicken and dumplings to pork chops—includes a vegetable. The perfect way to top off a meal is with a slice of homemade cream pie for seventy-five cents a slice. In the restaurant's Mural Room you can view paintings of historic and present-day sites in the Ironton-Arcadia Valley. Inexpensive prices. Open daily 6 A.M. to 9 P.M. Call 314-546-2719.

Ironton

Located about 2 miles (3.2 km) south of Pilot Knob on M-21, this town was founded in 1857 as the county seat of Iron County. It also has ties to the Civil War. A statue in front of the St. Marie du Lac Rectory, 350 South Main Street, commemorates the site where Ulysses S. Grant was appointed brigadier general. Grant made his headquarters here in 1861.

WHERE TO GO

Iron County Courthouse. 250 South Main Street. Right in the heart of town, this two-story structure is a good example of Greek architecture, particularly the cornices, entrance, and interior trim. Built in 1858, Union soldiers used it as a refuge when they retreated after the attack on Fort Davidson. The walls still bear the scars of Confederate gunfire. Open Monday through Friday 9 A.M. to 4 P.M.; Saturday 9 A.M. to noon. Call 314-546-2811.

St. Paul's Episcopal Church. 106 North Knob Street. This is a fine example of gothic architecture. After visiting this church and the courthouse, you may be hungry enough to mosey over to Kozy Korner or Grant's Inn for a bite to eat.

WHERE TO EAT

Kozy Korner. 201 South Main Street. Everything is home-cooked here from the biscuits and gravy to the pan-fried chicken, spaghetti, and dumplings. Make sure you try a slice of pie. You may have trouble choosing from the numerous varieties, but at these prices you can afford more than one piece. Open Monday through Saturday 6 A.M. to 7:30 P.M. Closed Sunday. Call 314-546-7739.

Grant's Inn. 375 South Main Street. This pleasant restaurant offers genuine competition to the Kozy Korner. Home-style lunches are served at inexpensive prices. The real specialty is the prime rib served on Fridays and Saturdays. If you dare, try a Missouri Mine Breaker, the house drink served by the pitcherful. Open Tuesday through Saturday 10 A.M. to 1:30 A.M.; Sunday noon to midnight. Call 314-546-9697.

Arcadia

One mile (1.6 km) south of Ironton on M-21 is the quaint town of Arcadia. Surrounded by swift mountain streams and quiet woodlands, the town provides the perfect location for people who wish to retreat from the world for a while.

WHERE TO GO

Royal Gorge. Located on M-21 about 5 miles (8 km) south of Arcadia. This scenic area, complete with roadside stop, boasts beautiful cliff formations that rise above the roadbed. Make sure you have your camera and film ready to record the highest peaks of the Ozarks.

Taum Sauk Mountain. Located at the end of County Road CC, 3 miles (4.8 km) west of M-21 and 6 miles (9.7 km) south of Arcadia. Taum Sauk rises 1,772 feet above sea level, making it the highest point in the state. Climbing to the top of the lookout tower provides you with an excellent view of the area.

You can explore the area firsthand on the Tom Sauk Trail. Only 1 mile (1.6 km) southwest of the mountain's crest is Mini Sauk Falls. With a cascade of 132 feet, it is the highest waterfall in the state. (You should try to time your visits to avoid dry spells.) According to legend, the falls were formed when an Indian chief was thrown from a high ledge for making love to Chief Taum Sauk's daughter, Mina Sauk, who leaped from the ledge to join her lover. The legend claims the Storm King struck the mountaintop with a bolt of lightning, causing water to flow down the gorge and wipe away the blood of the young lovers.

About ¾ mile (1.2 km) southwest of the falls lies the Devil's Toll Gate, an 8-foot-wide gap that is 50 feet long and 30 feet high. The historic military road that led to the Southwest Territory ran through the gate. Here, the Devil collected his "toll" in hard work and sweat—some wagon trains had to be unloaded and swung around the narrow passages by hand.

Taum Sauk Pumped Storage Plant. Located south on M-21. Turn west on to County Road AA until you reach Hogan, 12 miles (19.3 km) south of Arcadia. Then drive about 8 miles (12.9 km) on County Road AA to visit this engineering and scenic marvel.

The plant is actually located atop Proffit Mountain, where a reservoir was made by leveling the mountaintop. Water from

this upper reservoir flows down a 7,000-foot shaft and tunnel to
a powerhouse. It is pumped from a lower reservoir back to the
upper one when the power demand is low.

You can view the upper reservoir from an observation plat-
form. A Visitor's Center contains a scale model with a narration
on how the plant works. There's also the adjacent Taum Sauk
Nature museum, with displays of the state's natural resources
and geology. Open from March through November, daily 7:30
A.M. to 5:30 P.M. No admission fee. Call 314-621-3222, ext. 2817.

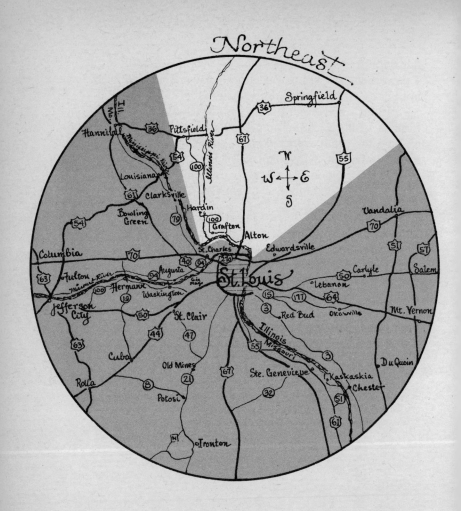

Northeast

NORTHEAST

DAY TRIP I

Springfield

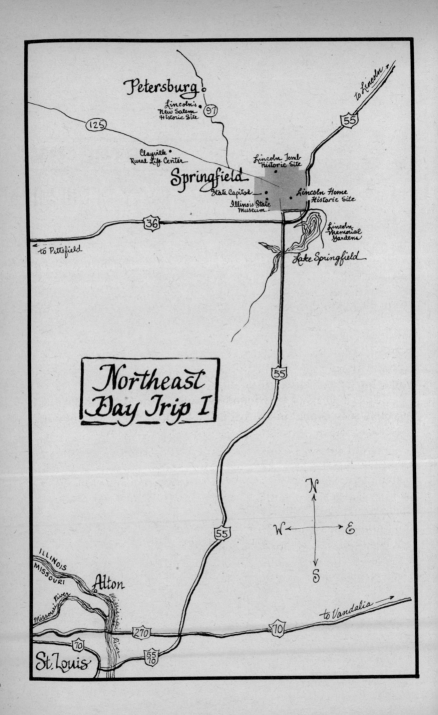

Petersburg

Lincoln's
New Salem
Historic Site

97

125

Clayville
Rural Life Center

Springfield

State Capitol

Illinois State
Museum

Lincoln Tomb
Historic Site

Lincoln Home
Historic Site

to Lincoln

55

Lincoln
Memorial
Gardens

Lake Springfield

36

to Pittsfield

55

Northeast
Day Trip I

N

W ——— E

S

55

ILLINOIS

MISSOURI

Alton

Missouri River

Mississippi River

to Vandalia

270

10

70

55
70

St. Louis

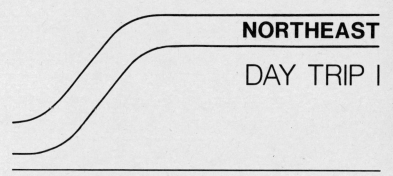

NORTHEAST
DAY TRIP I

SPRINGFIELD

Illinois is the Land of Lincoln, and nowhere is it more apparent than in Springfield, where Lincoln spent much of his legislative time before becoming president.

The town itself was founded back in the early 1800s and became state capital in 1837. It is filled with Lincoln landmarks, as well as many other noteworthy sites and historic homes.

To get there, take the quick and easy I-55 route north. The trip takes about three hours, a little longer than some of the other Day Trips, but the town and area are filled with a wealth of things to see and do. You may even decide to make it a two-day trip.

If you want more information, call the Springfield Convention and Tourism Commission at 217-789-2360.

WHERE TO GO

Lincoln Home National Historic Site. Eighth and Jackson streets. This was the only home Lincoln ever owned. It was built in 1839 and Lincoln bought it in 1844. It's been preserved in near-original condition, and many of the furnishings are original Lincoln family pieces. Eighth Street between Jackson and Capitol streets is closed to traffic, so you can explore here in car-free comfort. No admission fee. Call 217-525-4241.

Illinois State Museum. Spring and Edwards streets. Exhibits include anthropology, natural history, and geology. They also have a display by Illinois artists and artisans. No admission fee. Call 217-782-7386.

Lincoln Depot Museum. 930 East Monroe Street. Lincoln made his final address here before leaving to assume the presidency. It's now a museum with life-sized figures of Abe and Mary Todd Lincoln. Admission fee. Call 217-785-3856.

Lincoln Tomb State Historic Site. Oak Ridge Cemetery, about 2 miles (3.2 km) north of the capitol on Walnut Street. Lincoln's tomb is here, along with the grave sites of Mrs. Lincoln and three of their four children. Inside the tomb are small bronze statues representing different phases of Lincoln's illustrious career and bronze plaques contain the text of the Gettysburg Address and his Farewell Address. No admission fee.

Old State Capitol. Sixth and Adams streets. This was Illinois' fifth capitol site. Lincoln served his last legislative term here and delivered his famous "House Divided" speech in the Hall of Representatives. The capitol has been restored and is filled with original and reproduction furnishings that reflect the "way it was." No admission fee. Call 217-782-4836.

Illinois State Capitol. Second and Capitol streets. This is the current home of the Illinois legislature. The building was begun in 1867 and completed in 1888. Inside, murals and a bas-relief frieze decorate the dome. The first floor is open daily; guided tours are also available. No admission fee. Call 217-782-2099.

Vachel Lindsay Home. 603 South Fifth Street. Turn-of-the-century poet Vachel Lindsay lived here, and his manuscripts and drawings are now on display among period furnishings. Admission fee. Call 217-786-6789.

Lincoln's New Salem State Historic Site. 2 miles (3.2 km) south of Petersburg on IL-97. This is the reconstructed village where Lincoln spent six years in the 1830s. He worked as a storekeeper, surveyor, postmaster, budding lawyer, and finally a legislator. The cooper shop is the only original building at New Salem—this is where Lincoln did his studies at night. Cabins, shops, a carding mill, school, sawmill, gristmill, and the Rutledge Tavern have all been reproduced to reflect the town of Lincoln's youth. There's a museum here too, filled with (you guessed it) more Lincoln memorabilia. Picnicking and camping are available. No admission fee.

During the summer, a live production chronicles Lincoln's life and times. *Your Obedient Servant, A. Lincoln,* is presented every night except for Mondays. Admission fee. Call 217-632-7755.

Clayville Rural Life Center and Museum. 14 miles (22.5 km) west of Springfield on IL-125. This museum, run by Sangamon State University, features live re-creations of nineteenth-century rural life. The center was built around the Broadwell Tavern, a mid-1800s stagecoach stop. You can explore the blacksmith's shop, printer's shop, broom-maker's shop, and carpentry shop. The Broadwell Tavern is now called the Clayville Inn, but like everything else here, it is furnished in mid-nineteenth-century style. Admission fee. Call 217-626-1132.

Lake Springfield Park. From Springfield take Adlai Stevenson Drive east, turn south on East Lake Shore Drive, then make a sharp left onto West Lake Shore Drive. The park is 9,000-acres plus, 4,000 of which are Lake Springfield. You can boat, fish, camp, and generally have a good time here.

Take a drive down East Lake Shore Drive and view the 80 lakeside acres of the Lincoln Memorial Gardens, designed by landscape artist Jens Jensen.

WHERE TO EAT

Maldander's. 222 South Sixth Street. Elegant dinners upstairs, and breakfast and lunch downstairs. The restaurant is something of a historic landmark itself. It was built in the late 1800s. It's just 1 block south of Old Capital Plaza. Call 217-522-4313.

SPECIAL EVENTS

Illinois State Fair. Fairgrounds Park, Ninth and Sangamon streets. The biggest annual event in Illinois begins the first two weeks in August, but exact dates vary from year to year. It's billed as the largest agri-event in the nation, and along with the shows, harness racing, livestock judging, and tractor pulls, they also have an annual "husband-calling contest." Call 217-782-6661 for exact dates and information.

NORTHEAST

DAY TRIP II

Alton

Elsah

Grafton

Kampsville and Koster Site

Pittsfield

Batchtown

Brussels

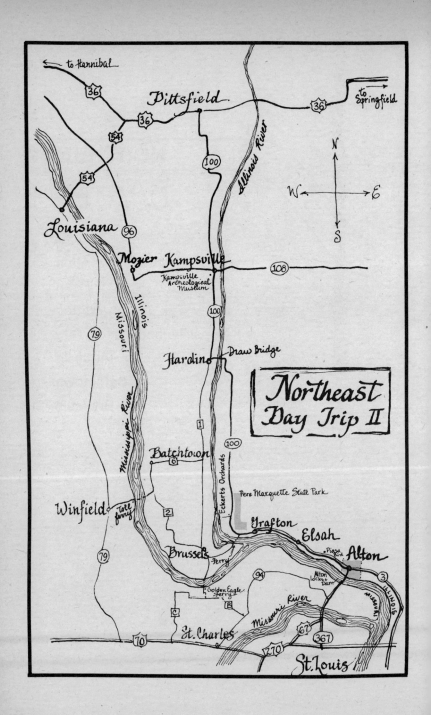

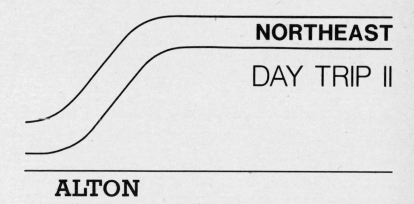

NORTHEAST
DAY TRIP II

ALTON

This Day Trip takes you north in Illinois along the Mississippi's Great River Road in the shadow of the limestone bluffs—reminders of the river's earlier depth.

Explorers Père Marquette and Louis Joliet passed by the Alton area in their 1673 voyage down the Mississippi. The first known settlers did not set up housekeeping until some 110 years after Marquette and Joliet paddled by. By the beginning of the nineteenth century, the town had become a thriving trading post and settlers began to build houses on the imposing hills and bluffs. Between 1816 and 1818, three different towns were founded in what is now known as Alton. One of these, now the central downtown business district, was planned by Col. Rufus Easton and named Alton for one of his sons.

Many of the elegant mansions built by early nineteenth-century residents still stand, beautifully restored, on the hilly Alton streets. Take a leisurely drive east of the downtown area on Henry Street to Ninth Street. This is known as "Christian Hill" and the homes in the area are lovely enough to cause you to search out "for sale" signs.

WHERE TO GO

Mansion House. 506 State Street. Built in 1834, this home served for 100 years as a lodging house. Although the house is not open to visitors, it's still worth a drive by to note the nineteenth-century charm.

Colonel Samuel Buckmaster House. 514 State Street. This three-story house was built between 1835 and 1850 and was owned by Col. Samuel Buckmaster, who served as the mayor of Alton in 1853 and again in 1862. The house is not open to the public.

Landmark's Visitors' Center. 119 Market Street. Tours of many other historic Alton homes are offered during the year. For information, stop by the center. Open Friday, Saturday, and Sunday 1 to 4 P.M. No charge for information. No telephone.

Elijah Lovejoy Monument. Fifth Street and Monument Avenue in the Alton Cemetery. Elijah Lovejoy was an ardent abolitionist and his newspaper made no bones about his stand against slavery. He was killed in 1837 while trying to protect his printing press from a pro-slavery mob. The monument commends his courageous actions.

Lincoln-Douglas Debate Marker. East Broadway at Market Street. The last debate between these two famous statesmen was held in the Alton City Hall, which stood at this site, less than 300 yards from the spot where Elijah Lovejoy was killed.

Piasa Bird. Located on the east side of the Great River Road about 4 miles (6.4 km) north of Alton. The Piasa Bird is one of Alton's most persistent legends. Marquette first described it in his journal as a painting on the high river bluffs of hideous monsters "as large as a calf, with head and horns like a goat; their eyes red; beard like a tiger; and face like a man's." The

Indians painted the original, but it was destroyed long ago by road construction and rock quarrying. It has been reproduced as close as possible to the original location.

Alton Locks and Dam. Just off Broadway near the foot of IL-67 bridge. You can see what those huge barges have to go through to get from one end of the Mississippi to the other. It's a relaxing treat to stand on the observation deck and watch as the water in the lock is adjusted to permit the barges to pass. Open dawn to dusk daily. Free.

SHOPS

Antiques lovers and dedicated browsers can spend an entire day searching Alton's many shops. Hours vary widely and are at the daily discretion of the shop owners. There are so many shops, however, that no matter what day you visit, you should find some open. The best advice is to call ahead. The most concentrated grouping of shops is along Broadway in the downtown district. Here is a sample of what awaits you:

The Pine Door. 207 East Broadway. This shop specializes in beautifully refinished antique furniture. It also has a good selection of glassware, lamps, and non-antique brass accent pieces at reasonable prices. Open Thursday and Friday 11 A.M. to 4 P.M.; Saturday and Sunday 11 A.M. to 5 P.M. Call 618-462-8945.

Steve's Antiques and Stripping. 323 East Broadway. If you don't have your heart set on real antiques, you might find a less expensive reproduction here that fits the bill. Steve's also has some authentic antique furniture as well as beautiful wall clocks and cast-aluminum furniture. Open Thursday through Monday 11 A.M. to 4 P.M. Call 618-465-7404.

Mini-Mall Antiques. 205 East Broadway (upstairs). There are several shops in this walk-through mall, but they are open only on weekends.

WHERE TO EAT

Tony's. 312 Piasa Street. This is a dinner restaurant that began 30 years ago peddling pizzas and has since become a favorite for steak-lovers. Pizzas are still a popular menu choice—they sell 400 to 500 a week at moderate prices. Open every day at 4 P.M. Call 618-462-8384.

FOR BIKERS ONLY

The Great River Road is also the Great Bike Path. About 1 mile (1.6 km) north of Alton there is a parking area specifically for bikers. You can park, unhitch your bike and head north on a well-marked and maintained path along the Great River Road all the way to Père Marquette State Park if your legs hold out for the full 20 miles—32.2 km. If not, just go as far as you can. On nice days, it can be fairly crowded, but courtesy is the order of the day and there's a pleasant camaraderie among bikers with aching muscles and sore derrieres. Free.

ELSAH

Several people thought Addison Greene had an idea whose time had come in 1847. He moved to this spot on the Mississippi north of Alton on the great River Road and began selling cord-wood to passing steamboats. Eventually, others moved here too. It was called Jersey Landing back then, but in 1853 Gen. James Semple saw a good prospect for river commerce, so he bought the area and renamed it Elsah. He developed the community by giving a house lot to any settler who would build a stone house there. Those sturdy stone houses still stand, making a vis-it to Elsah akin to traveling upriver to a nineteenth-century sea-port. The stone houses are still in good condition, their character enhanced by generations of families. The residents of this village always seem to be smiling and they welcome the city folk to the quiet life among the bluffs.

WHERE TO EAT

Elsah Landing. 18 LaSalle Street. This trip is worthwhile for just one bite of the Landing's famous lemon pie, or the mystery pecan pie. There are delicious homemade soups and sandwiches (which they call grinders) that come in whole or half sizes. If you aren't hungry when you visit, buy some of their homemade bread or rolls for later. Inexpensive prices. Open Tuesday through Sunday 11:30 A.M. to 7:30 P.M. Call 618-374-1607.

GRAFTON

As you continue north on the Great River Road between the Mississippi and the towering bluffs, you will pass through Grafton, located at the confluence of the Illinois and Mississippi rivers. In 1834, the town had one store, one tavern, and "a number of families." It was owned by James Mason, who optimistically predicted his town would become the chief river port of Illinois. While Grafton didn't live up to Mason's predictions, it still has some interesting sights to visit.

If you haven't tired of antiques, there are three shops right along Main Street as you drive through town: The Golden Eagle Antiques (call 618-786-3333); Mickie Finn Antiques (call 618-786-3385); and Tara Point (call 618-786-3555).

Once past the business district, you'll come upon some rather unusual houses at the river's edge. It's not that the builders thought they were "above" everyone else, they just wanted to build their houses out of reach of the frequently flooding river—so they built them on stilts.

WHERE TO GO

Eckerts Orchards. Turn right off the River Road on to Route 100 and go up the hill to Otterville Road, where you turn left. The orchard is about 1½ miles (2.4 km) after you turn. Look for the big red barn. In the spring, you can pick your own strawberries right off the vine and in late summer and early fall the staff takes customers into the orchard, where they can fill their own 20-pound sack with scrumptious apples. There is also a small shop on the grounds where you can buy cider, jams, jellies, and apple butter. Or, you can take your pickin's home and make your own. Call 618-786-3445.

Père Marquette State Park. About 5 miles (8 km) west of Grafton on the Great River Road. This 7,500-acre park, named for the early Mississippi explorer, has literally everything a camper or sightseer could desire. Horseback riding is available; there are miles and miles of hiking trails along the wooded bluffs, plus dozens of picnic and camping sites. It's open year round, but if you want to camp during the winter, you'll have to bring your own water. The lodge near the park entrance offers family-style cooking that includes a variety of daily specials. If you forget your tent, stay in one of the lodge's cabins or motel rooms. The restaurant is open year round, daily 8 A.M. to 8 P.M. No admission fee to the park. Call 618-786-3351 (lodge); 618-786-3323 (park information).

KAMPSVILLE AND KOSTER SITE

Continuing north on IL-100 toward Hardin, the scenery retains its wilderness beauty as you pass through more and more fertile farmland. At Hardin you will cross the area's only drawbridge over the Illinois River (be careful to watch the warning lights if you don't want to take an untimely swim). Then drive on to Kampsville. The Koster Archeological Site, said to be one of the oldest in North America, was discovered near here in 1969 and has helped put this tiny town on the map. Although the Koster site has been closed, there are two other working sites nearby open to visitors:

Audrey Site. If you are traveling north on IL-100, turn right at the Eldred/Hillview Road and proceed for about 5 miles (8 km). The site, located in an open field, is open to visitors from March until the end of October, Monday through Friday 8 A.M. to 4 P.M.

Ansell-Knight Site. This one is right on IL-96 just south of Mozier.

Both sites were discovered in the late 1960s. For help in finding either site, stop by the Northwestern University Archeology office in Kampsville. There is no address, but you can find it near the Kampsville ferry dock right between the town's two restaurants (Kampsville Inn and Circle Inn). If you want a guided tour, write to Ellen Gantner, Director of Admissions, Box 1499, Evanston, IL 60204, or call her at 312-492-5300. There is a fee for a guided tour. There is no fee for other visitors.

WHERE TO GO

Kampsville Archeological Museum. Just on the left of IL-100 as you enter Kampsville. The museum, which is located in what used to be the town meat market, has exhibits of the many archeological finds from the area. Open Memorial Day to Labor Day, daily 9 A.M. to 5 P.M. Donations accepted. Call 618-653-4614.

The Old Village Church. Look for the yellow steeple across the street from the museum and you'll find this shop. It is full of knickknacks, reproduction oak furniture, curio cabinets, oak tables and chairs, handmade toys, quilts, brass pieces, and lots of glassware. Open Monday through Saturday 10 A.M. to 4 P.M. ; Sundays noon to 5 P.M. Call 618-653-4508.

PITTSFIELD

If you don't want to return to Missouri via a ferry ride, you may continue north through Illinois on IL-100 to Pittsfield, one of America's largest pork-producing areas. As you drive into town you'll see the spire above the Pike County Courthouse, a three-story building erected in 1894. The small hog on the courthouse lawn is a little monument to the area's largest industry.

From Pittsfield you can take one of several routes back home—depending on your mood and your time. You can return via IL-36 west to Hannibal and drive back on the Missouri side of the river. IL-36 to IL-54 south takes you across the bridge to Louisiana, Missouri. You can also drive back through the towns of Batchtown and Brussels and catch a ferry across the Mississippi or Illinois rivers.

WHERE TO EAT

Red Dome Restaurant. 125 East Washington Street in Pittsfield. This place is famous for its tasty inch-thick pork tenderloin dinner, which includes salad, potato, rolls, and beverage at a reasonable price. The pork tenderloin sandwich is also a good buy. Open Monday through Saturday 6 A.M. to 9:30 P.M. Call 217-285-6502.

BATCHTOWN

Head south on IL-100 to Hardin and take County Road 1 south. Along the way you'll pass giant bluffs to your right and corn-filled valleys to your left on this peninsulalike region flanked by three rivers: Illinois, Mississippi, and Missouri.

Calhoun County is a lush, bountiful place that's traditionally been a favorite with apple growers. The high ridges between the Illinois and Mississippi rivers help keep the climate temperate in late winter and early spring, which prevents the young budding trees from freezing. If you keep your eyes open along this route during late summer and early fall, you'll see several roadside fruit stands brimming with apples.

At the intersection of County Roads 1 and 6, head west over a wonderful hilly stretch of road that loads to Batchtown. When you reach it, you'll see a sign directing you to turn left. Go 2 miles (3.2 km) down this narrow country road, take a gravel turnoff to the Winfield ferry, which travels the Mississippi River between Calhoun County and Winfield, Missouri. You can cross here for $3 a car year round, weather permitting, from early morning until 8 P.M. If you get lost, just ask a friendly Batchtown resident for directions.

WHERE TO EAT

Apple Shed Restaurant. The road that takes you to the Winfield ferry also takes you to the Apple Shed Restaurant. The sign at the turnoff says the ferry is 2 miles (3.2 km) and the restaurant is 1 mile (1.6 km) so you can stop for a bite before you cross the river to Missouri. They've got homemade turtle soup and pork chop dinners. On Sundays, you can sample fried chicken and roast beef buffet (all you can eat) at inexpensive prices. The restaurant is located inside a real apple shed built in 1934. It's open from noon on Fridays, Saturdays, and Sundays. Groups can call ahead to make arrangements for meals during the week. Call 618-396-2681.

BRUSSELS

Head south on County Road 2 and take the turnoff left over

high ridges and breathtaking views until you reach Brussels. You may take the free Brussels ferry across the Illinois River, in case you want to continue your travels in an easterly direction. The ferry doesn't have a lot of old-time atmosphere, but it is fast, efficient, and runs 24 hours a day, seven days a week, river conditions permitting. On nice afternoons, there's usually about a 15-to-20-minute wait.

The town itself is built on the prosperity of the area's agricultural ventures—especially its apple orchards.

At the Wittmond Hotel and General Store, you can stop for lunch, for a snack, or for the night at one of the state's best-known country inns. It was built in 1847 and served as a rest stop for the overland stagecoaches that passed this way. It is open every day from 11:30 A.M. to 7 P.M. The red brick building sits on the right side of the road as you enter Brussels. Call 618-883-2345.

If you really want to treat yourself, don't miss the *Golden Eagle* ferry, an honest-to-goodness paddle-wheel ferry that has the feel of Mark Twain Country about it. Drive south from Brussels about 6 miles (9.7 km). When you come to the proverbial "fork in the road" stay to the right and follow the signs to the ferry. The cost is $3.50 per car for the ride across the Mississippi to Missouri, where you can head back to St. Charles. The ferry operates from May 1 to December 15; weekdays 8 A.M. to 7 P.M.; weekends until 9 P.M. Call 618-883-2217.

There's only one drawback to this ride: the ferry gets plenty of business day and night, so be prepared to wait up to an hour to cross. However, you may park your car in line and walk to Kinder's Restaurant adjacent to the dock. Here you can get a drink and a sandwich and park the kids in the game room. Or, if you're really hungry, stay and have a fresh catfish or chicken dinner. The place is open late on weekends. Call 618-883-2586.

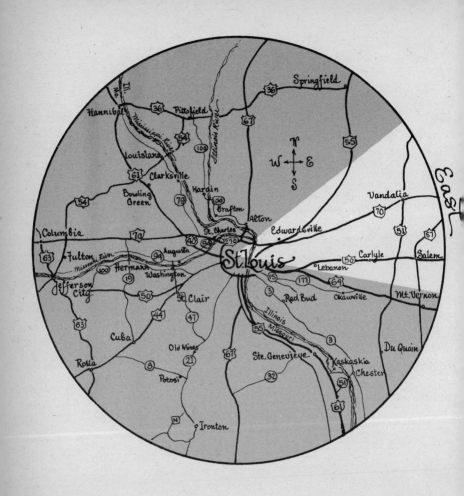

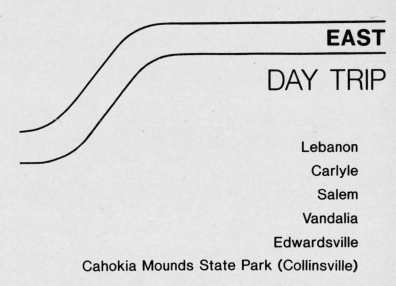

EAST
DAY TRIP

Lebanon

Carlyle

Salem

Vandalia

Edwardsville

Cahokia Mounds State Park (Collinsville)

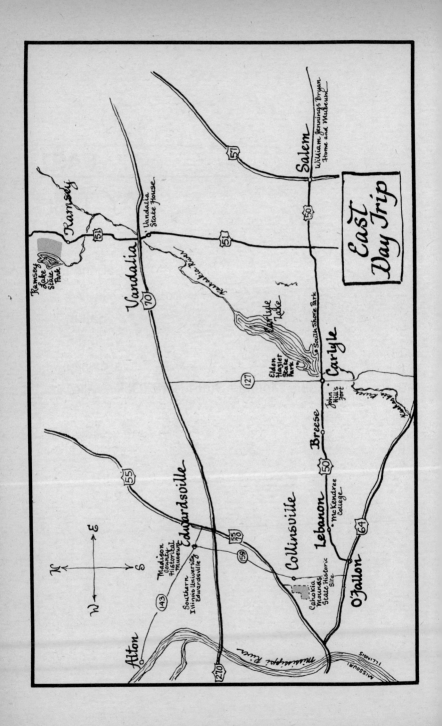

East Day Trip

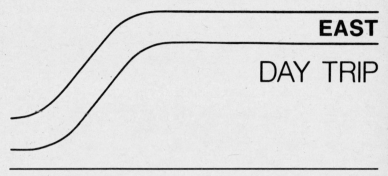

LEBANON

Taking U.S. 50 east, you'll reach Lebanon, in St. Clair County. It is one of the oldest settlements in this region of southern Illinois. Laid out in 1814, its main street looks much the same today as it did back in the late 1800s, with wooden sidewalk awnings and well-preserved brick storefronts. If you are searching for some quiet inspiration, stop for a moment at the McKendree College chapel. It is on the shaded grounds of the college, which began as a Methodist seminary in 1828.

CARLYLE

The seat of Clinton County is located east on U.S. 50. It is the site of John Hill's Fort, erected to protect early settlers from Indian attacks. Treasure hunters can take heart in the local legend of a settler named Young, who was killed and buried near the fort. His mother declared she had sewn $5,000 into his clothes, but dedicated attempts to find the body and its bounty have proved fruitless.

WHERE TO GO

Lake Carlyle. Just off IL-50 east of town. This 25,000-acre lake is Illinois' largest and the pickings are good for anglers looking for a dinner of largemouth bass, walleye, or catfish. The most popular fishing spot seems to be in the Kaskaskia River just at the foot of the dam that created this man-made lake. On its 85 miles (136.8 km) of shoreline, there are swimming beaches, boat docks, launching areas, and boat rentals. Call 618-594-4637.

Eldon Hazlet State Park. 1351 Ridge Street, Carlyle. There are 372 camping spots to choose from here and if you get tired of the lake, you can explore the hiking trails and admire the bluffs. You can also take in the view from the observation point. Open year round. Call 618-594-3015.

South Shore State Park. RR 3, Carlyle. This park is on the opposite shore from Eldon Hazlet; it is also open year round. There are only 33 campsites here, but the view of the lake is just as nice as from Hazlet. Call 618-594-3015.

Gen. William F. Dean Suspension Bridge. Fairfax and First streets, just downstream from the dam. Walk across the only suspension bridge still standing in Illinois. It was built in 1859 and used for 70 years. Before the bridge was built travelers had to cross the Kaskaskia by ferry or mud bridge. It was later dedicated to William F. Dean, a Carlyle native and a Korean war hero. No toll fee.

SALEM

From Carlyle, continue east on U.S. 50 to Salem. Salem was settled in 1813 on what used to be the Vincennes–St. Louis

stagecoach route (now known as IL-50). In addition to its agricultural heritage, it was once a major oil-producing area. In
1940, around 295,000 barrels were produced each day. Some oil
is still produced here.

WHERE TO GO

William Jennings Bryan Home and Museum. 408 South Broadway. The three-time Democratic presidential nominee was born
in this two-story frame house on March 19, 1860. His home is
now a museum filled with personal effects, family furnishings,
letters, and other memorabilia. Open Saturday through Wednesday. Admission fee.

VANDALIA

From Salem, head back west on U.S. 50 to U.S. 51 and drive
north to Vandalia, the second capital of Illinois (Kaskaskia was
the first). Abraham Lincoln received his license to practice law
here and he along with his opponent Stephen A. Douglas
served a portion of their legislative years at the Vandalia State
House. The 6-block area around the State House bears bronze
markers commemorating the many historical sites of Vandalia.

WHERE TO GO

Vandalia State House. 315 Gallatin Street. The three-story brick
building took only four months to build in 1836, at a cost of
$16,000. Both Stephen A. Douglas and Abraham Lincoln spent
their formative legislative years on opposite sides of the House
of Representatives meeting room. The imposing white brick
building with its tall columns and green lawn is furnished in
period style, reminiscent of the days when Lincoln and Douglas

walked these halls. Open daily 9 A.M. to 5 P.M. No admission fee. Call 618-283-1161.

Madonna of the Trail. On the statehouse lawn. This statue stands as a monument to the pioneer mothers who trudged the Cumberland Trail.

WHERE TO EAT

Jay's Barn Restaurant. 730 West Gochenour Street. For dinner, you can eat fried catfish with soup or salad, vegetable, or potato for about $6. There are also good steaks and sandwiches. Daily lunch specials cost about $3. They serve breakfast every day from 6 A.M. Open daily until 9:30 P.M. Call 618-283-2585.

Abe Lincoln Cafe. Gallatin and Fourth streets, just across from the Vandalia State House. For $4.95 on Sundays you can sample the buffet here. Open daily 5:30 A.M. to 8 P.M. Call 618-283-9794.

EDWARDSVILLE

To reach Edwardsville from Vandalia, take I-70 west to IL-159 and head north. The seat of Madison County, Edwardsville was founded in 1813 and incorporated in 1837. The town was named after Ninian Edwards, governor of the Illinois Territory from 1809 to 1818. Through the years, Edwardsville has proven a popular spot for Illinois governors—eight of them have lived here at one time or another.

WHERE TO GO

Madison County Historical Museum. 715 North Main Street.

This Federal-style brick house was built in 1836 and is now filled with Indian artifacts and relics of Illinois' pioneer predecessors. Open Wednesday through Friday 9 A.M. to 4 P.M.; Sunday 1 to 4 P.M. No admission fee. Groups should make advance reservations. Call 618-656-7562.

Southern Illinois University—Edwardsville. This 2,600-acre campus on the western edge of Edwardsville has an enrollment of about 11,000 students. But you don't have to be a student to take advantage of many of the programs. Art exhibits, special senior citizen presentations, films, recitals, and concerts are held year round and are open to the public. To find out what's coming up, call the University Information Center at 618-692-2739 weekdays 8 A.M. to 5 P.M.

CAHOKIA MOUNDS STATE PARK (COLLINSVILLE)

Heading south on I-55 from Edwardsville, take I-70 southwest to IL-157 and Collinsville. Incorporated as a village in 1856 and as a city in 1872, Collinsville is named for William Collins, one of five brothers who established the settlement. Not far from town is the Cahokia Mounds State Historic Site, which many believe is the only prehistoric Indian city north of Mexico.

WHERE TO GO

Cahokia Mounds State Historic Site. To reach the site (not to be confused with the town of Cahokia) catch I-55 and I-70 west toward St. Louis and get off at the Cahokia Mounds exit. The site's address is 7850 Collinsville Road. Here you'll see over 100 mounds used for ceremonial activities by Indians that first inhabited the area around A.D. 700. By A.D. 900 this site had become the regional center for the Mississippian Indian culture. Monks Mound, the largest of the mounds, is reputed to be similar in size to the Great Pyramid of Egypt. Call 618-344-5268.

The museum is open year round, daily 9 A.M. to 5 P.M. You may want to examine the variety of exhibits about aspects of prehistoric life. There is even a full-scale model of an Indian hut and garden. From June through August, archeologists are busy excavating and visitors are welcome to watch and ask questions (8 A.M. to 10 P.M.). No admission fee. Camping is also available, as are picnic tables and barbecue pits. Group tours can be arranged by calling 618-344-5268 in advance of your visit.

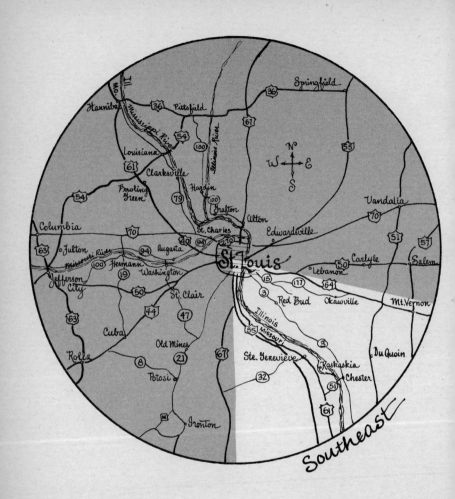

SOUTHEAST

DAY TRIP I

Belleville

Okawville

DuQuoin

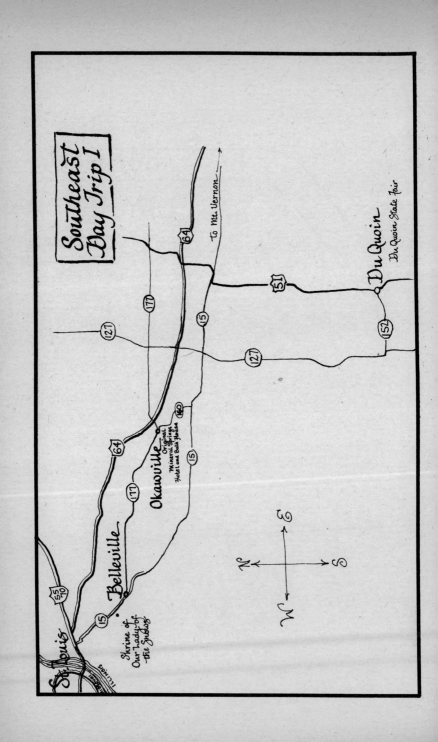

Southeast Day Trip I

St. Louis

55 70

ILLINOIS

15

Shrine of
Our Lady of
the Snows

Belleville

64

177

Okawville
Original
Mineral Springs
Hotel and Bath Houses

160

15

64

177

121

15

127

15

64

To Mt. Vernon

51

127

Du Quoin
Du Quoin State Fair

152

N

E

S

W

Named for the chief of the Kaskaskia Indian tribe, Jean Baptiste DuQuoigne (an Indian of French extraction), this town is an important cog in the southern Illinois coal-mining machinery. But the town is probably more famous for the annual Du-Quoin State Fair, with its big-name entertainment, booths, and shows. The fair used to be home of the Hambletonian, the Kentucky Derby of harness racing, but the event has since moved to Middletown. has replaced it with a rival race—the World Trotting Derby. The 11-day fair always ends on Labor Day and the race is held on the last Saturday of the fair. Admission fee. Call 618-542-5484.

At the end of June, DuQuoin also hosts the Farm and Folk Festival on the fairgrounds. The highlight of the festival, which includes crafts demonstrations and lots of food, is the Illinois Championship Cowchip Tossing Contest.

For information, call 618-542-5484.

SOUTHEAST

DAY TRIP II

Cahokia

Columbia

Waterloo

Red Bud

Prairie du Rocher

Chester

Kaskaskia Island

Ste. Genevieve

Crystal City / Festus

Herculaneum

Kimmswick

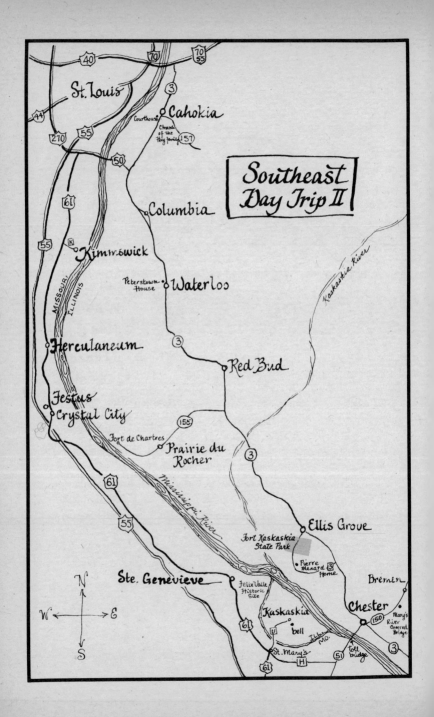

Southeast
Day Trip II

St. Louis
Cahokia
Courthouse
Church of the Holy Family
Columbia
Kimmswick
Peterstown House
Waterloo
Herculaneum
Red Bud
Festus
Crystal City
Fort de Chartres
Prairie du Rocher
Ellis Grove
Fort Kaskaskia State Park
Pierre Menard Home
Ste. Geneviève
Felix Valle Historic Site
Kaskaskia
bell
Brémen
Chester
Mary's River Covered Bridge
St. Mary's
toll bridge

MISSOURI
ILLINOIS

Mississippi River
Kaskaskia River

N
W   E
S

SOUTHEAST

DAY TRIP II

The Great River Road follows the Big Muddy through Illinois as well as Missouri. This scenic Day Trip will take you through Illinois' historic French Colonial District.

CAHOKIA

This trip is one that may be taken in two parts, beginning in Illinois with Cahokia and stopping for the night at Ste. Genevieve in Missouri, and then continuing home the next day.

From St. Louis, take I-70 across the river and head south on IL-3 to one of the state's most venerable towns. Through the years it has been slowly surrounded by East St. Louis's industrial development, but there are still remnants of days gone by.

Cahokia started as a summer camp of the Tamaroa Indians. Missionaries from the Seminary of Foreign Missions visited in 1698 and by 1699 Jean François Buisson de St. Cosme had completed a house and chapel—the first church in Illinois. Jesuit missionaries soon followed and the two orders disagreed on which mission had jurisdiction. The area was ceded to the British in 1765 and to the United States in 1778, but the flavor here is still decidedly French.

WHERE TO GO

Church of the Holy Family. 4 miles (6.4 km) south of I-70 at the intersections of IL-3 and IL-157. Built on the site of the original mission church, this log house of worship was completed in 1799. It has been in continuous use during French, British, and American rule. Well-meaning parishioners covered the original walnut log walls with clapboard, but it has now been restored and was named a National Historic Landmark in 1971. Behind the church, take a walk through the Cahokia cemetery where you can find the graves of Indians, French colonists, and slaves. Call 618-337-4548.

Cahokia Courthouse. 112 Main Street (just off IL-3). Built as a residence in the mid 1700s, the structure became the courthouse in 1793. The stone and log building was dismantled and reassembled in St. Louis for the 1904 St. Louis World's Fair and then moved again to Chicago. It came home in 1938 when the original site was excavated, and the courthouse was reconstructed according to old photographs and early sketches. No admission. Call 618-332-1782.

COLUMBIA

The original German settlers might not recognize the town they founded in 1866, but to visitors Columbia still has the sturdy, wholesome feeling associated with those early settlers. To get to Columbia, take the Main Street turnoff at IL-3. It will take you through town and back to IL-3, where you can continue your trip south.

WHERE TO EAT

Eberhard's Stein Museum and Restaurant. 117 North Main Street. Here's a good selection of German food at reasonable prices. And if you aren't in the mood for Wiener schnitzel, the restaurant also has American selections. Lots of German beer in stock here. A large collection of steins are exhibited in an authentic "Bierstube." Open Tuesday through Saturday 5 to 10 P.M. ; Sunday 11:30 A.M. to 10 P.M. Call 618-281-5400.

WATERLOO

On your drive south on IL-3 from Columbia to Waterloo, you will pass several two-story brick farmhouses. Some are white-washed, others are surrounded by prim picket fences, and all are a visual reminder of gracious farm life from an earlier era.

Waterloo was settled on the old trail leading from Fort de Chartres to Cahokia. In the early 1900s the town was a haven for young lovers seeking wedded bliss. Competition among local justices of the peace was quite fierce until stricter marriage laws were passed in 1937.

On your way through town, take time to slow down and admire the town square, courthouse, and beautifully preserved turn-of-the-century buildings.

WHERE TO GO

Peterstown House. On North Main Street just to your right as you enter Waterloo on IL-3. This white frame two-story house with its trim green shutters was a popular stop for stagecoaches traveling from Fort de Chartres to Cahokia. The house is named for Emery Peter Rogers, an astute businessman who started with 5 acres in the early 1800s. He soon owned everything from a woolen mill and general store to a brickyard, quarry, and carriage factory. The house has been restored and furnished. Open Saturday and Sunday 1 to 5 P.M. No admission fee.

RED BUD

It's a pleasant drive south on IL-3 from Waterloo to Red Bud past more picturesque farms and fertile farmland. This town is named, in case you couldn't tell, for the red bud trees that flourish in the area. The beautiful wrought iron balconies on Main Street are reminiscent of those found in New Orleans.

PRAIRIE du ROCHER

The oldest town in Illinois, Prairie du Rocher was officially founded in 1722. Before that, the area was occupied by missions, forts, and trading posts. It is still a tiny village—only 650 residents. To reach it from IL-3, turn west on to the southern branch of the Lincoln Heritage Trail (IL-155) and wend your way through the wooded hillside until you reach the town. If you visit during New Year's, you may think you've stepped into a time machine. The villagers still celebrate the New Year with the traditional "La Guiannee"—a French custom in which townspeople don costumes and masks for dancing and singing.

WHERE TO GO

Fort de Chartres. 4 miles (6.4 km) west of Prairie du Rocher. When Pierre Duque de Boisbriant arrived here in 1718, he thought this site near the Mississippi River would make an ideal location for the permanent military post he had been commissioned to command. Unfortunately, de Boisbriant did not reckon with the eccentric habits of the Mississippi, which soon flooded the wooden fort. It was rebuilt in 1727 with the same result. In 1732, the army had finally learned something of the Mississippi's character, so they moved the fort to the northwest and farther from the river. It too was doomed to dilapidation. But in 1751, the engineer in charge decided to change the course of fate. He chose a site between the first two locations and ordered construction of a snug and (he hoped) attack-proof stone fort. It was substantially completed by 1756, and later earned the reputation for being "the best-built fort in North America."

Today, many of the original stone buildings still stand. Some have been reconstructed, and visitors can get a cordial taste of history as they walk through the 18-foot-high stone entryway that leads to the main fort compound. During the summer there are crafts demonstrations every weekend. Each June, a "Rendezvous" re-creates the crafts and contests of these early settlers. You can sample French pastries, homemade breads, preserves, and hardy stews. The Rendezvous also highlights military pageantry. The French Marines, French Village Militiamen, and Royal Highland Regiment don colorful period costumes and act out the roles of their eighteenth-century predecessors. Open daily 9 A.M. to 5 P.M. No admission fee. Call 618-284-7230.

La Pelleterie. Fort de Chartres. During the heyday of the French Colonial District, the trading post at Fort de Chartres was a major stop for traders, hunters, and area settlers. Today Pat and Karalee Tearney operate La Pelleterie in the best tradition of the first trading posts. They sell a variety of historical reproductions from lanterns, candlesticks, and candle snuffers to German silver or brass snuffboxes, pipes, and knives. But their specialty is costumes—not the kind you buy for Halloween—the kind you find in the best museums.

Before constructing a period costume to your specifications, they thoroughly research the styles and designs taken from original period artwork. They make every effort to obtain materials as close to the original as possible. Open April through October, daily, except Monday, 10 A.M. to 5 P.M. ; from November through March, open Wednesdays through Saturdays 10 A.M. to 5 P.M. "in good weather." Call ahead for an appointment or a catalogue of their wares. Call 618-284-7171 or 618-826-4334.

Fort Kaskaskia Historic Site. Located just off IL-3, near Chester. Bring plenty of color film when you visit this historic area overlooking the confluence of the Mississippi and Kaskaskia rivers. Spring sunsets are spectacular. This once was the site of the old French fort of Kaskaskia, built in 1736, rebuilt in 1761, and then destroyed in 1767 to prevent occupation by approaching British troops. Garrison Hill and Menard cemeteries, both located here, contain the remains of 3,800 bodies that were moved from Kaskaskia Island (see p. 170) when the 1881 flood created the island. Camping is available. No admission fee.

Pierre Menard Home. Just past the Fort Kaskaskia Historic Site entrance off IL-3. Built in 1802 by the first lieutenant governor of Illinois, this French colonial home was called the "Mt. Vernon of the West." The home is a remarkable study in restoration. Many of the furnishings belonged to the Menard family; the rest are authentic period pieces. Open year round except Thanksgiving, Christmas, and New Year's Day, daily 9 A.M. to 5 P.M. No admission fee. Call 618-859-3031.

CHESTER

The county seat of Randolph County was founded in 1819 by a Cincinnati, Ohio, firm that wanted to establish a commercial rival to the thriving town of Kaskaskia. To reach Chester from Fort Kaskaskia, you can take County Road 3 east to IL-3 and head south.

Named after the English town of Chester, this town is the final resting place for Shadrach Bond, first governor of Illinois. Probably the most famous character to come out of Chester was not Bond, but a cartoon caricature named Popeye. Elzie Chrisler Segar, Popeye's creator, was born here in 1894. Popeye was based on Segar's recollections of Frank "Rocky" Fiegel, a local "scrapper" he had known in his youth. A statue commemorating this famous Chester character stands at the entrance to the toll bridge (sixty-cent fee) that takes you across the river to Missouri.

WHERE TO GO

Mary's River Covered Bridge. Take IL-3 south through Chester and turn left (northeast) on IL-150 toward Steelville. The bridge is about 7 miles (11.3 km) from Chester on the right-hand side of the road. It opened in 1854 as part of the plank toll road between Bremen and Chester. Back then it cost only $530 to build this 70-foot bridge. It was a popular haunt for highway robbers, who found stagecoaches easy prey. No toll fee.

KASKASKIA ISLAND

To get here, you must travel across the Chester toll bridge to Missouri, drive north on County Road H to St. Mary's and then cross the bridge over the shallow channel. This is the only part of Illinois located west of the Mississippi! Old Kaskaskia was the first capital of Illinois. It was opened as a Catholic mission in 1703, four years after Cahokia was founded. In 1881, the Mississippi flooded and cut a new course through old Kaskaskia, making it an island. There is a state memorial here and a brick building houses the bell that rang every Sunday at the Church of the Immaculate Conception. It is known as the "Liberty Bell of the West" because villagers rang it on July 4, 1778, after receiving word that France had joined the War of Independence. It is 11 years older than its sister in Philadelphia and the two share a common characteristic: both are cracked. It is rung every July 4 to commemorate America's independence.

STE. GENEVIEVE

After your visit to Kaskaskia Island, cross the bridge back to St. Mary's and continue the second half of your journey. Traveling north on U.S. 61 it's a short distance to Ste. Genevieve, the oldest settlement in Missouri. Plan to spend some time here—perhaps stay the night in order to take in the many wonderful homes, shops, and restaurants that are part of the town's eighteenth- and nineteenth-century charm.

Ste. Genevieve was settled by the French in 1726, nearly 40 years before Pierre Laclède founded a trading post in St. Louis. In fact, Laclède visited St. Genevieve in 1763 during his journey up the Mississippi in search of a profitable location for a river trading post. Historians speculate that if Laclède hadn't found a housing shortage in Ste. Genevieve, it would have claimed the prominence awarded to St. Louis!

Preservation and restoration efforts here prove that dedication and a lot of hard work can save America's pioneer heritage. The government recognized the town's historic value in 1976 when it named the downtown area an official "Historic District." To reach this area, turn left on Market Street from U.S. 61 and drive for about 1½ miles (2.4 km) on what used to be the Old Plank Road. The architecture echoes the influence of the town's French, Spanish, and German heritage. Many of its restored homes and buildings are open to the public. For information on organized tours, call the Civic Tour Service at the museum at 314-883-3461. Before you start your tour of Ste. Genevieve, stop by the Tourist Center at Third and Merchant streets. Call 314-883-5750.

WHERE TO GO

Ste. Genevieve Museum. Merchant Street at DuBourg Place. According to one of the city's most durable legends, Jesse James emptied the Ste. Genevieve Savings and Loan safe on May 26, 1873. True or not, that safe is on display here, along with several birds mounted by John James Audubon during his stay here. There are also many Indian relics and some historical documents on display. Open April through November, daily 9 A.M. to 4 P.M. ; November through April, daily noon to 4 P.M. Admission fee. Call 314-883-3461.

Ste. Genevieve Catholic Church. DuBourg Place at Merchant Street, across from the museum. It took the town from 1876 to 1880 to build this church, and its spire is a landmark. It is the third church building to occupy this corner, where the town's first Catholic church was erected in 1752. Services are held on Saturdays at 4:30 P.M. and 7 P.M. ; and on Sunday mornings at 6:30, 8:30, 10, and 11:30.

Felix Valle Historic Site. Merchant and Second streets. This house was built in 1818. Felix and Odile Pratte Valle lived here and ran the office for Felix's fur, lead, and iron business out of their home. It is open to visitors only during the annual Jour de Fête held the second weekend in August. Call 314-883-7102.

Guibourd-Valle House. North Fourth and Merchant streets. This white house with its wide, airy front porch was built in 1785 by Jacques Jean René Guibourd, who first moved to Ste. Genevieve in 1780. The house is an excellent example of the "they don't make them like they used to" tradition. It is a vertical log construction on a rock foundation. If you venture up the winding stairway to the spacious attic, you can admire the methods of the early builder who joined hand-hewn log beams together with sturdy wooden pegs. The wolf could have huffed and puffed himself into the next county and not blown this house down.

In the early 1930s, Jules Felix Valle bought the house and restored it. He and his wife furnished it with family heirlooms, and when she died in 1973, her will stipulated that the house and its furnishings be left to the city. As you leave, stroll through the formal gardens at the rear of the house. The two gravestones do not mark graves of Guibourd or Valle relatives: Mrs. Valle considered her two dogs as family and they are buried here. Open Monday through Sunday 10 A.M. to 5 P.M. Admission fee. Call 314-883-7544.

Beauvais House. Main and Merchant streets. The original settlers of Ste. Genevieve built their homes closer to the river. But the annual floods, the worst in 1785, forced the residents to move 4 miles (6.4 km) inland, to the present site of the town. This house was built in 1770 in the old settlement and moved to its present site in 1785. Open in the winter, daily 10 A.M. to 4 P.M. ; in the summer, daily 10 A.M. to 5 P.M. Admission fee.

Green Tree Tavern. 244 St. Mary's Road. Built in 1790, this house served as an inn and tavern after the Louisiana Purchase. The unique triangular fireplace warms three rooms. Open Monday through Saturday 10 A.M. to 5 P.M. ; Sunday 10 P.M. to 4 P.M. Admission fee.

Bolduc-Le Meilleur House. Market and Main streets. This

house, erected in 1820, is an example of the American influence on French architectural styles in Ste. Genevieve. Open June through September, Monday through Saturday 10 A.M. to 4 P.M.; Sunday 11 A.M. to 4 P.M. Closed in winter. Admission fee.

Bolduc House. 125 South Main Street. Located next door to the Bolduc-Le Meilleur House, this home was built in the 1770s and moved to this site in 1784. It is considered to be the most authentically restored Creole-style building in America. The stockade fence, frontier kitchen, and eighteenth-century garden help one visualize what life was like for Missouri's early settlers. Open April 1 to November 1, Monday through Saturday 10 A.M. to 4 P.M.; Sundays 11 A.M. to 4 P.M. Admission fee. Call 314-883-3105.

Amoureaux House. ½ mile (.8 km) east of U.S. 61 on St. Mary's Road. An excellent example of French colonial architecture, this home built in the 1770s has been lovingly preserved. After you admire the antique furnishings and doll collection, visit the Country Store in the rear and pick out a memento of your trip. Open in the winter 10 A.M. to 4 P.M.; in the summer 10 A.M. to 5 P.M. Admission fee. Call 314-883-5744.

Linden House. Main street just across from the Bolduc House. This house, not open to the public, was named for the rare linden tree in the yard. It was built between 1800 and 1805 and is now owned by the Missouri Chapter of the National Society of Colonial Dames of America.

Dr. Benjamin Shaw House and Fur Trading Post. Second and Merchant streets. These two buildings were constructed around 1790 and the Shaw house was modernized around 1850. Several fixtures and doors in the Shaw house were taken from a riverboat that was wrecked near Ste. Genevieve. The trading post and slave quarters are connected to the main house by a stone corridor, where some examples of regional art are displayed. Ste. Genevieve was once a thriving artists' colony and the house's current owner is one of the last of these artists. You have to knock on his garden gate for entrance, but he will be glad to show you around and tell you about the town's history. Admission fee. Call 314-883-2319.

Memorial Cemetery. Fifth and Market streets. To truly appreciate the town's historic heritage, take an afternoon stroll among the headstones that immortalize the town's earliest settlers. Graves here date to the late 1700s. No admission fee. Closes at dusk.

ANTIQUES

Jeanne's Under the Varnish Antiques. 188 North Main Street. This shop stocks furniture and glassware. Open Saturday 10 A.M. to 5 P.M.; Sunday 10 A.M. to 6 P.M. Hours can vary, so call ahead at 314-883-3514.

Little French Hen. 252 Market Street. The shop features work by Missouri artists. It also has a selection of antiques and crafts. Hours and phone number are available at the Tourist Center, Third and Merchant streets, 314-883-5750.

Mary Jane's Antiques. 73 North Main Street, across from St. Gemme Beauvais. The shop owner's specialty is repairing dolls, and she carries quite a selection. You can also find gifts, china, and furniture. Call 314-883-5838.

Monia's U-Save Mart. 316 Market Street. Looking for the perfect gift for a baby, wedding, or housewarming? This shop has a huge selection of handmade quilts at reasonable prices. It also carries hardware, greeting cards, and quilting supplies. Open Monday through Saturday 8 A.M. to 5:30 P.M. Closed Sunday. Call 314-883-5820.

MARKETS

John Oberle Meat Market. 950 Ste. Genevieve Road (also known as U.S. 61). This family has been known for its sausages and meats since the present owner's grandfather first opened shop in 1870. The sausage is homemade from a secret family recipe. The market recently added cheese to its inventory. Open Monday through Saturday 8 A.M. to 7 P.M. ; Sunday 2 to 8 P.M. Call 314-883-3379.

Jack Oberle Market. M-32 about 1 mile (1.6 km) west of town. This is another of the famous Oberle meat shops featuring homemade sausage and delicious cheese. Open Monday through Saturday 7 A.M. to 5 P.M. Closed Sunday. Call 314-883-5656.

WHERE TO EAT

Old Brick House. Third and Market Streets. In addition to a heritage of delicious food, this restaurant is also well known because it is believed to be the oldest brick building west of the Mississippi. It was built around 1790 and served as the first district courthouse. Today's guests can relax in the tavern or restaurant amid the nineteenth-century furnishings and enjoy a delicious fried catfish dinner. On Sundays you can feast on fried chicken served family style. The restaurant also serves a meal guaranteed to fill up the hungriest diner: a 40-ounce steak dinner with all the trimmings. It can either be divided among four people or served to one person with a hollow leg. You'll get super food here, at super prices. Open Monday through Thursday 8 A.M. to 9 P.M. ; Friday and Saturday 8 A.M. to 10 P.M.; Sunday 11 A.M. to 8 P.M. Call 314-883-2724.

Anvil Restaurant. 46 South Third Street. The elegantly carved antique backbar is this restaurant's decorative focal point. Ceiling fans, sturdy oak tables, and rustic brick walls also create a nineteenth-century air, which is the era when this building was first constructed. The menu is not extensive, but the food is good, hot, and reasonably priced. Open Monday through Saturday 11 A.M. to 10 P.M. Closed Sunday. Call 314-883-7262.

The Inn Ste. Gemme Beauvais. 78 North Main Street. If you plan to spend the night in Ste. Genevieve, by all means do it here. This three-story inn was built in the 1840s and its 18-inch walls were meant to withstand the wear and tear of many generations. There are six two-room suites and two guest rooms, all equipped with private baths. A French breakfast is included in the price of a room, which is $30 for a double. During the summer, lunch is served in the Victorian dining room and is open to guests as well as other visitors. Reservations for an overnight stay are recommended. Open year round. Call 314-883-5744.

Oberle's Restaurant. U.S. 61, next to the meat market. In addition to homemade sausage selections, the menu here includes steaks and fried chicken. Daily lunch specials are cheap. Open Monday through Friday 7 A.M. to 10 P.M. ; Saturdays 8 A.M. until 11:30 P.M. Closed Sunday. 314-883-9757.

SPECIAL EVENTS

Jour de Fête. Each year, on the second weekend in August, Ste. Genevieve holds a festival to celebrate the town's many firsts—first settlement in Missouri, first tavern (The Green Tree), first convent, and first brick house.

You can take the historic homes tour, sample the wares of Missouri's artisans at the arts and crafts show and applaud the variety of street entertainers that range from German bands to Indian dancers. Call 314-883-5609.

CRYSTAL CITY/FESTUS

These two sister cities on U.S. 61 north of Ste. Genevieve owe their success to the Mississippi sand that dominates the area. A group of visiting surveyors found what they thought was an unusual grade of sand at this settlement. It turned out to be sand that is highly prized in the production of plate glass. By 1872 the American Plate Glass Company had begun to build a factory here, and a town known as "New Detroit" sprouted up around this fledgling industry. Because of the nature of the business, the townspeople promptly nicknamed their town Crystal City. The name stuck.

Residents of "New Detroit," or Crystal City, were not allowed to drink alcohol near the factory or town by order of the factory owners. American ingenuity and capitalism recognized that another settlement was necessary. A few miles away another city began to grow; this one had saloons. The town was first known as Tanglefoot, then Limitville, and finally, Festus. Some say it was named to honor a St. Louis banker, Festus J. Wade. The more romantic believe the name was chosen by a visiting preacher who opened his Bible to a random passage and pointed at the name "Festus" in the Book of Acts. Whichever, "Festus" was incorporated in 1888.

WHERE TO GO

Pittsburgh Plate Glass Co. (now known as PPG Industries). 26 Mississippi Avenue in Crystal City. This company bought out the Crystal Plate Glass Company in 1906, and if you want to see how they make the stuff that lets light into your living room and keeps the rain out, take a tour of the factory. You must call the main office in Festus for reservations. Tours are available Monday through Friday. 314-937-3621 (extension 223).

HERCULANEUM

This tiny town, on U.S. 61 north, was the first county seat of Jefferson County. It started out as a shipping point for the lead mined a few miles south. In 1808, Moses Austin and Samuel Hammond laid out a plan for the town and named it for a village in southern Italy that was buried in the eruption of Mt. Vesuvius in A.D. 79.

Religious history is Herculaneum's main claim to fame. Before 1804, when the United States gained control of this territory from the Spanish, the Roman Catholic Church was the only religion permitted in the area. No Protestant ministers were allowed to serve here. But as Spain's control of the area began to dwindle, Protestant preachers began to cross the Mississippi River from Illinois to lead Protestant worship services. The first of these, according to legend, was preached in Herculaneum by Rev. John Clarke in 1798. An art glass window at the Herculaneum Methodist Church, 200 North Main Street, commemorates this historic event. Call 314-479-3385.

KIMMSWICK

The Great River Road leads you back of St. Louis on U.S. 61.

The town of Kimmswick, 20 miles (32.2 km) south of St. Louis, is about 1 mile (1.6 km) east of U.S. 61 on Route K. It was laid out in 1859 by German immigrant Theodore Kimm, for whom the town was named. It was very prosperous after the Civil War and early rail and river transportation sparked many successful businesses. The Montesano Park recreation resort opened in the 1800s and wealthy St. Louisans soon adopted Kimmswick as a popular weekend resort. An excursion steamer made several trips down the Mississippi each day. But superhighways passed the town by and boats and trains no longer stopped there. Buildings began to deteriorate as businesses left the area.

In 1970, Lucianna Gladney Ross sparked a restoration project in Kimmswick, giving the town a new lease on life. Today, several buildings and homes dating to the mid-1800s have been restored. Seven of these are included on a Kimmswick homes tour, which can be arranged by calling Eileen Mohan at 314-464-0296. If you visit Kimmswick during one of the three annual festivals (see listing on pages 172 and 173), the homes will be open for viewing.

WHERE TO GO

Burgess How Museum. Third and Elm streets. This beautifully restored building was the first to be moved to Kimmswick for the restoration. Built in the 1840s, it was the home of the Edward S. How family and stood on route Z in Mapaville. It is open to the public in the spring and summer on Sundays 2 to 5 P.M. Admission fee.

SHOPS

Many of Kimmswick's shops are open only on weekends. Call for an appointment during the week.

A Is for Apple. Second Street. This quaint shop was opened by a former schoolteacher who also serves as the official spokesperson for Kimmswick events. The shop is open Tuesdays, Thursdays, and weekends. For information on Kimmswick events or on the shop's hours, call Helen Smart, 314-467-3020.

The Arnold House. Elm Street. This combination antique and craft shop is open on Tuesdays, Thursdays, and weekends. For information call 314-467-1157.

The Country Store. Market and Second streets. This shop was built by Michael Ziegler in 1913. It has a nice variety of antiques. Open only on weekends; other days by appointment. No phone.

Captain's Corner Antiques. Front and Market streets. Built in 1877, this store is located in what used to be The Market. Through the years, it has been a general store, meat market, tavern, and home. Today, it specializes in restored antiques. Open on weekends 11 A.M. to 4:30 P.M. Call 314-772-3006.

WHERE TO EAT

The Old House Restaurant. Second and Elm streets. This fine restaurant is operated by the Kimmswick mayor, Georgia Crow. The log building was constructed in 1770 near Arnold and was moved to Kimmswick in 1973. There was a tavern in one wing of the building and stagecoach drivers used to stop regularly to rest the horses and quench their thirst. You don't have to arrive in a stagecoach to sample the excellent food. Dinners include prime rib, barbecue rib dinners, fried chicken, and roast beef. Open only on weekends: Friday and Saturday 5 to 9 P.M.; Sunday noon to 9 P.M. Call 314-464-0378.

The Blue Owl. Second Street at Mill. A charming, reasonably priced restaurant located in a restored nineteenth-century tavern, this find is open for lunches Monday through Friday from 11 A.M. until 2 P.M. It is operated by the owners of the Old House Restaurant. For information, call 314-464-0378.

SPECIAL EVENTS

Summer Festival. Held each year at the beginning of June. There are lots of activities, ranging from arts and crafts demonstrations to square dancing and a greased-pig-catching contest. You can also tour the restored homes. Admission fee. 314-467-3020.

Candelight Tour. Held the first Sunday in December to celebrate the Christmas season. The restored homes are decorated and the guides dress in period costumes to give the holiday an air of antiquity. There is a fee for the tour. Call 314-467-3020.

Apple Butter Festival. Held the last weekend in October. Homemade apple butter is the highlight of this annual event. It usually runs out by Saturday afternoon, but the homes are still open to visitors on Sunday. Admission fee. Call 314-467-3020.

DAY TRIP
DIRECTORY

Restaurants

Hotels, Inns, and Motels

Campgrounds

State Parks

Historic Sites

Celebrations and Festivals

Additional Information

Travel Information

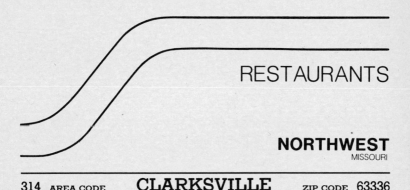

RESTAURANTS

NORTHWEST
MISSOURI

314 AREA CODE **CLARKSVILLE** ZIP CODE 63336

Duvall Restaurant. M-79, across from Skylift Country Cooking. 242-9680

314 AREA CODE **BOWLING GREEN** ZIP CODE 63336

Chum's Restaurant. 30 miles (48.3 km) south of Bowling Green at U.S. 61 and M-47 in Troy. Moderately priced country cooking. 528-6121.

314 AREA CODE **HANNIBAL** ZIP CODE 63401

Country Kitchen of Hannibal. U.S. 61 N. Fast food, family prices. 221-8441.
Mark Twain Dinette. Third and Hill streets. Hearty dinners. 221-5300.
Ole Planter's Restaurant. 316 N. Main St. Italian food is the rule in a full-service restaurant where checks average under $10. 221-4410.
Ponderosa. Huck Finn Shopping Center. Family prices. 221-2874.

314 AREA CODE **LOUISIANA** ZIP CODE 63353

Li'l Henry's. U.S. 54 at M-79 and the bridge. Good fried chicken and catfish. 754-3116.
The Olde-Hotel Restaurant. 125 S. 3rd St. Family prices. 754-5411.

WEST

314 AREA CODE	**COLUMBIA**	ZIP CODE 65201

Ernie's Steak House. 1005 E. Walnut St. 874-9455. See p. 24 for more restaurant listings in Columbia.

314 AREA CODE	**KINGDOM CITY**	ZIP CODE 65262

Gasper's Restaurant. U.S. 54 at I-70. 642-6641.

314 AREA CODE	**ST. CHARLES**	ZIP CODE 63301

St. Charles Vintage House & Wine Garden. 1219 S. Main St. Overlooks the Missouri River. Located in the Historic District of St. Charles. 946-7155.
Noah's Ark Restaurant. I-70 at 5th St. exit. 946-1000.

See p. 15 for more restaurant listings in St. Charles.

SOUTHWEST

314 AREA CODE	**ARCADIA**	ZIP CODE 63621

Andy's Restaurant. M-72 & M-21. 546-2573.

314 AREA CODE	**AUGUSTA**	ZIP CODE 63332

Ivy La Point's Farmer's Hotel. Soups, sandwiches, and desserts. 228-4410.

---

314 AREA CODE   **CUBA**   ZIP CODE **65453**

Noel Picard Midway Lounge & Restaurant. 101 E. Washington St.
885-3980.

---

314 AREA CODE   **DE SOTO**   ZIP CODE **63020**

Gannon's Cafeteria. 48 Jefferson Sq. Shopping Center. 586-6665.

---

314 AREA CODE   **EUREKA**   ZIP CODE **63025**

Friar Tuck's. 115 W. 5th St. (N. Service Rd.) at I-44. 938-5880.

---

314 AREA CODE **FREDERICKTOWN** ZIP CODE **63645**

Continental Restaurant. U.S. 67 S. 783-2938.

---

314 AREA CODE   **HERMANN**   ZIP CODE **65041**

The Calico Cupboard. 4 Schiller St. 486-2030.
Concert Hall Bar and Barrel. 206 First St. 486-9989.
Vintage 1847 Restaurant. Next to Stone Hill Winery. 486-3479.

---

314 AREA CODE   **HILLSBORO**   ZIP CODE **63050**

Hillsboro Restaurant. Specializes in homemade breads and pies.
Courthouse Sq. 789-2216.

---

314 AREA CODE   **IRONTON**   ZIP CODE **63650**

Kozy Korner. 201 S. Main St. Home-cooked food. 546-7739.
Grant's Inn. 375 S. Main St. Home-style lunches. 546-9697.

314 AREA CODE   JEFFERSON CITY   ZIP CODE 65101

State House Restaurant. 216 Madison St. 635-6514.
Oscar's Steak House. 1441 Christy Lane. 636-8124.

314 AREA CODE   MARTHASVILLE   ZIP CODE 63357

Green Gable Restaurant. On M-47. 433-5533.

314 AREA CODE   PILOT KNOB   ZIP CODE 63663

Fort Davidson Cafe. Has full-service dining room and coffee shop. 546-2719.

314 AREA CODE   POTOSI   ZIP CODE 63664

Ken's Dine-In. M-21 at the junction of M-8 in the Parkway Shopping Center. 438-2474.
Kennon Cafe. 117 E. High. 438-4921.

314 AREA CODE   ST. CLAIR   ZIP CODE 63077

Lewis Cafe. In the heart of town at 145 S. Main St. 629-9975.

314 AREA CODE   ROLLA   ZIP CODE 65401

Zeno's Steak House. Two locations: Martin Spring Dr. in Rolla; and I-44, N. Service Lane in Sullivan. 364-1301 and 468-4121 respectively.
Howard Johnson Restaurant. Business 44 & 66. 364-9847.

314 AREA CODE   STANTON   ZIP CODE 63079

The Windmill Restaurant. At I-44; visible S of the interstate. 927-5291.

| 314 AREA CODE | STEELVILLE | ZIP CODE 65565 |

Big T Restaurant. At M-19 in Steelville. 775-2770.

| 314 AREA CODE | WASHINGTON | ZIP CODE 63090 |

The Embers Restaurant. 602 W. 5th St. 239-3334.
Elijah McClean's. 600 W. Front St. 239-4404.

| 314 AREA CODE | WASHINGTON STATE PARK | ZIP CODE 63664 |

Thunderbird Dining Lodge. Take in the scenery of the Big River. 586-6696. Open April 15 to October 31.

| 314 AREA CODE | WESTPHALIA | ZIP CODE 65085 |

Westphalia Inn. Main St. Fried chicken and country ham dinners served family style. 455-9991.

NORTHEAST
ILLINOIS

| 618 AREA CODE | ALTON | ZIP CODE 62002 |

Ramada Inn. 1900 Beltline. Family-style dining is offered at all three meals a day. 463-0800.
Tony's. 312 Piasa St. 462-8384.

---
618 AREA CODE   **BATCHTOWN**   ZIP CODE **62006**

Apple Shed Restaurant. 1 mile from the turn-off to the road that leads to the Winfield Ferry. Homemade soup and pork chop dinners. 396-2681.

---
618 AREA CODE   **BRUSSELS**   ZIP CODE **62013**

Brussels Restaurant & Tavern. 883-2233.
Kinder's Restaurant. 6 mi (9.7 km) S of Brussels. 883-2586.
Wittmond Hotel. Once a stage stop, now a hotel with a general store. Highly regarded for its country cooking. 883-2345.

---
618 AREA CODE   **ELSAH**   ZIP CODE **62028**

Elsah Landing. 18 LaSalle St. in the heart of town. As charming as the town around it. Pull off the Great River Rd. (IL-3) for soup, sandwich, homemade breads, and pies at lunch and dinner. 374-1607.

---
618 AREA CODE   **GRAFTON**   ZIP CODE **62037**

Great River Road Inn. 511 W. Main St. Family-style prices and food at lunch and dinner. 786-3838.
Père Marquette Lodge. In Père Marquette State Park on the Great River Rd. (IL-3). Famous for fish. Enjoy breakfast, lunch, or dinner in a rustic setting situated just off the enormous lobby of the lodge. 786-3351.

---
618 AREA CODE   **HARDIN**   ZIP CODE **62047**

The Barefoot. A restaurant/bar on the Illinois River just N of Hardin, where the specialty is catfish and river fish. 576-9002.
Royce's Restaurant. Caters to businesspeople; serves plate lunches. 576-9092.

| 618 AREA CODE | HARTFORD | ZIP CODE 62048 |

Hartford Cafe. 1 S. Market St. 254-7126.

| 618 AREA CODE | KAMPSVILLE | ZIP CODE 62053 |

Kampsville Inn Restaurant. 653-4413.
Circle Inn Restaurant. 653-9602.

| 217 AREA CODE | PITTSFIELD | ZIP CODE 62363 |

Red Dome Restaurant. 125 E. Washington. 285-6502.

| 217 AREA CODE | SPRINGFIELD | ZIP CODE 62703 |

Maldander's. 222 S. 6th St. 522-4313.

EAST

| 618 AREA CODE | BREESE | ZIP CODE 62230 |

Wally's Malt Shop. 711 N. 4th St. 526-7893.

| 618 AREA CODE | CARLYLE | ZIP CODE 62231 |

Crystal Chandelier Restaurant & Bakery. 981 Fairfax St. For breakfast or lunch. No phone number listed with information.
West Access Marina. Carlyle Lake Rd. Order all day from breakfast, lunch, or dinner menus. 594-2461.

---

618 AREA CODE   **SALEM**   ZIP CODE **62881**

White Brick. 1110 W. Main St. Family-style prices at all three meals. 548-9887.

---

618 AREA CODE   **VANDALIA**   ZIP CODE **62471**

Abe Lincoln Cafe. Gallatin and 4th Sts. 283-9794.
Jay's Barn. 730 W. Gochenour St. 283-2585.
Mabry Motel Restaurant & Cafe. 1502 N. 8th St. Open daily 6 A.M. to 10 P.M. 283-0588.

SOUTHEAST
ILLINOIS/MISSOURI

---

618 AREA CODE   **COLUMBIA**   ZIP CODE **62236**

Eberhard's Stein Museum & Restaurant. 117 N. Main. 281-5400.

---

618 AREA CODE   **DuQUOIN**   ZIP CODE **62832**

Emling's Cafe. 9 E. Main St. Serves breakfast, lunch, and dinner. 348-8260.

---

314 AREA CODE   **KIMMSWICK**   ZIP CODE **63053**

The Old House Restaurant. 2nd & Elm sts. 464-0378.

---

618 AREA CODE   **MURPHYSBORO**   ZIP CODE **62966**

Elsie's Cafe. 1842 Walnut. Serves breakfast, lunch, and dinner. 684-4180.

---

618 AREA CODE   **OKAWVILLE**   ZIP CODE **62271**

Original Mineral Springs Hotel. 506 Hanover St. Come for the night or for a day at the bathhouse, or stay for a meal. 243-5458.

---

618 AREA CODE **PRAIRIE du ROCHER** ZIP CODE **62277**

LePetit Buffet. Market St. Have breakfast, lunch, or dinner. 284-3444.

---

618 AREA CODE   **RED BUD**   ZIP CODE **62278**

Wright Place. 1064 S. Main St. Fast food. 282-7991.

---

314 AREA CODE   **STE. GENEVIEVE**   ZIP CODE **63670**

Anvil Restaurant. 46 S. 3rd St. 883-7262.
Cafe Genevieve. N. Main & Merchant sts. 883-2737.
The Inn Ste. Gemme Beauvais. 78 N. Main St. Dine in and spend the night. A French breakfast is included with the price of a room. 883-5744.
Old Brick House. 3rd and Market sts. A 40-ounce steak dinner with all the trimmings. 883-2724.
Oberle's Restaurant. U.S. 61 next to John Oberle Meat Market. 883-9757.

For more restaurants, see p. 132.

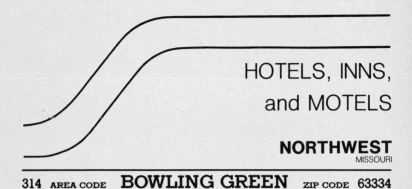

HOTELS, INNS, and MOTELS

NORTHWEST
MISSOURI

---

314 AREA CODE **BOWLING GREEN** ZIP CODE **63334**

Princess Motel. U.S. 54 & U.S. 61. 324-3241.

---

314 AREA CODE **CLARKSVILLE** ZIP CODE **63336**

Best Western Duvall Motel. 2nd & Lewis sts. on M-79. 242-3511.

---

314 AREA CODE **ELSBERRY** ZIP CODE **63343**

Hillcrest Motel. 1 mi (1.6 km) N of Elsberry on M-79. 898-2121.

---

314 AREA CODE **HANNIBAL** ZIP CODE **63401**

Hannibal House Best Western. 3603 McMasters Ave. 46 rooms. 221-7950.
Holiday Inn. U.S. 61 S at Market St. 245 rooms. 221-6610.

---

314 AREA CODE **LOUISIANA** ZIP CODE **63353**

River's Edge Motel. 201 Mansion St. (U.S. 54). 754-4522.

151

---

314 AREA CODE   **TROY**   ZIP CODE **63379**

Turnbull Motel. 2 blocks off U.S. 61 in Troy. 582-4400.

WEST

---

314 AREA CODE   **COLUMBIA**   ZIP CODE **65201**

Best Western Downtown University Center. 1111 E. Broadway. 102 rooms. 449-2401.
Ramada Inn Columbia. 1100 Vandiver Dr., I-70 & U.S. 63 N. 205 rooms. 449-0051.
Tiger Motor Hotel. 23 S. 8th St. 100 rooms. 449-4121.

---

314 AREA CODE   **FULTON**   ZIP CODE **65251**

Travelier Motel. 600 U.S. 54 S. 642-3332.
Pine Crest Motel. Business U.S. 54 N. 642-6043.

---

314 AREA CODE   **ST. CHARLES**   ZIP CODE **63301**

Howard Johnson's West. 1425 S. 5th St. at I-70. 150 rooms and a 24-hour restaurant. 946-6936.
Noah's Ark Motor Inn & Restaurant. I-70 at 5th St. exit. 180 rooms. 946-1000.

---

314 AREA CODE   **WENTZVILLE**   ZIP CODE **63385**

Best Western Heritage Motel. 404 N. U.S. 61, on Business 61. 54 rooms. 327-6263.

SOUTHWEST

---

314 AREA CODE   **CUBA**   ZIP CODE **65453**

Wagon Wheel Motel. 901 E. Washington St. 885-3411.

---

314 AREA CODE   **EUREKA**   ZIP CODE **63025**

Holiday Inn–Eureka–Six Flags. I-44 at Eureka exit. 199 rooms and a Holidome. 587-7000.

---

314 AREA CODE **FREDERICKTOWN** ZIP CODE **63645**

The Corral Motel. 5 mi (8 km) S of Fredericktown exit on U.S. 67. 783-3352.

---

314 AREA CODE   **GRAY SUMMIT**   ZIP CODE **63039**

Daniel Boone Motel. On M-100 near I-44. 742-4146.

---

314 AREA CODE · **HERMANN**   ZIP CODE **65041**

Der Klingerbaunn Inn. 108 E. 2nd St. 486-2030.
German Haus Motel. 113 Market St. Built in 1847. 486-2222.
Hermann Motel. ½ mi (.8 km) S of town on M-19 at 112 E. 10th St. 486-9991.

---

314 AREA CODE   **IRONTON**   ZIP CODE **63650**

Mimosa Hotel. On M-21. 546-7418.

---

314 AREA CODE **JEFFERSON CITY** ZIP CODE **65101**

Capital Best Western. 1937 Christy Lane. 83 rooms. 635-4175.
Holiday Inn Downtown. 422 Monroe St. 165 rooms. 636-5101.
Ramada Inn. 1510 Jefferson St. 235 rooms. 635-7171.

| 314 AREA CODE | **LESTERVILLE** | ZIP CODE **63654** |

Wilderness Lodge. M-21 S to Wilderness Lodge/Riversedge sign at jct. of M-49 & M-72, then W to Peola Rd., and turn S on Peola Rd. A rustic retreat on the Black River, complete with cottages, fireplaces, a main lodge, and dining room. Packed lunches available. Activities galore in the summer. St. Louis toll free 296-2011 or 637-2295.

| 314 AREA CODE | **PILOT KNOB** | ZIP CODE **63663** |

Fort Davidson Motel. 1 mi (1.6 km) N of Ironton. 546-7427.

| 314 AREA CODE | **POTOSI** | ZIP CODE **63664** |

Potosi Hotel. 215 E. High St. 438-9094.
Lone Star Motel. 403 N. Missouri St. 438-9002.

| 314 AREA CODE | **ST. CLAIR** | ZIP CODE **63077** |

St. Clair Motel. 1 mi (1.6 km) W of St. Clair on Old Hwy. 66. 629-2109.

| 314 AREA CODE | **ST. JAMES** | ZIP CODE **65559** |

Country-Aire Motel. 3 mi (4.8 km) W of St. James on N. Outer Rd. 11 units. 265-8151.

| 314 AREA CODE | **STANTON** | ZIP CODE **63079** |

Meramec Caverns Motel. Adjacent to Meramec Caverns, 3 mi (4.8 km) S of exit 230 off I-44. 468-4215.

| 314 AREA CODE | **STEELVILLE** | ZIP CODE **65565** |

Eagle Hurst Ranch. Star Rte. 288, Box 35, Steelville. 786-2625.
Rainbow Courts. On M-19. 775-2450.

---

314 AREA CODE   **SULLIVAN**   ZIP CODE **63080**

Sullivan Motel. S. Outer Rd. 468-4117.

---

314 AREA CODE   **WASHINGTON**   ZIP CODE **63090**

Jasper's Motel. 436 Elm St. 239-2949.

NORTHEAST
ILLINOIS

---

618 AREA CODE   **ALTON**   ZIP CODE **62002**

Stratford Motel Hotel. 1 block off U.S. 67 & IL-3 downtown at 229 Market St. 465-8821.

---

618 AREA CODE   **BRUSSELS**   ZIP CODE **62013**

Wittmond Hotel & General Store. 883-2345.

---

618 AREA CODE   **ELSAH**   ZIP CODE **62028**

Maple Leaf Cottages. No. 12 Selma St. 374-1684.

---

618 AREA CODE   **GREENVILLE**   ZIP CODE **62246**

Bel-Air Motel. I-70 & IL-127 at exit 45. 664-1950.

---

618 AREA CODE   **HARDIN**   ZIP CODE **62047**

Hardin Hotel. 576-9003.

---

618 AREA CODE   # KAMPSVILLE   ZIP CODE **62053**

Kampsville Inn, Restaurant-Bar & Hotel. 653-9605.

---

217 AREA CODE   # SPRINGFIELD   ZIP CODE **62703**

Bel-Aire Manor Motel. Business I-55 (2636 S. 6th St). 544-1783.

Best Rest Inn. Bypass 66 (700 N. Dirksen Pkwy.). Zip code 62702. 522-7961.

Days Inn. Stevenson Dr. exit off I-55 (3000 Stevenson Dr.). 529-0171.

Holiday Inn East. I-55 at Stevenson Dr. exit (3100 S. Dirksen Pkwy.). 529-7171.

Springfield Travelodge. Business I-55 downtown (500 S. 9th St.), across from Lincoln Home. Zip code 62701. 528-4341.

State House Inn Best Western. 101 E. Adams St. Zip code 62701. 523-5661.

EAST

---

618 AREA CODE   # BREESE   ZIP CODE **62230**

Knotty Pine Motel. U.S. 50 W. 526-4556.

---

618 AREA CODE   # CARLYLE   ZIP CODE **62231**

Carlyle Motel. U.S. 50 & IL-127. 594-2444.

Motel Carlyle. Fairfax St. & IL-127. 594-2445.

---

618 AREA CODE   # COLLINSVILLE   ZIP CODE **62234**

Holiday Inn. 475 N. Bluff Rd. Near the intersection of I-55, I-70, & IL-157. 345-9000.

Roundtable Best Western Motor Lodge. I-55 & IL-157. 345-5660.

---

618 AREA CODE   **EDWARDSVILLE**   ZIP CODE **62025**

Holiday Inn. I-270 & IL-157. 656-3000.

---

618 AREA CODE   **GRANITE CITY**   ZIP CODE **62028**

Chain of Rocks Motel. I-270 & IL-3. 931-1100.

---

618 AREA CODE   **SALEM**   ZIP CODE **62881**

Lakewood Motel. U.S. 50 E. 548-2785.

---

618 AREA CODE   **VANDALIA**   ZIP CODE **62471**

Robbins Best Western Motel. I-70 & U.S. 51 (N. 8th St.). 283-2112.

SOUTHEAST

---

618 AREA CODE   **BELLEVILLE**   ZIP CODE **62222**

Hyatt Lodge. 2100 W. Main St. 234-9400.

---

618 AREA CODE   **CARBONDALE**   ZIP CODE **62901**

Holiday Inn of Carbondale. IL-13 (800 E. Main St.). 457-2151.

---

618 AREA CODE   **CAHOKIA**   ZIP CODE **62206**

Trails End Motel. 600 Water St. (IL-3). 332-9719.

---

618 AREA CODE   **CENTRALIA**   ZIP CODE **62801**

Langenfeld Hotel. 104 W. Broadway. 532-7315.

---

618 AREA CODE   **CHESTER**   ZIP CODE **62233**

Royal Motor Lodge. 1012 State St. 826-2341.

---

618 AREA CODE **MOUNT VERNON** ZIP CODE **62864**

Regal 8 Inn. I-57 & U.S. 460. 244-2383.

---

618 AREA CODE **MURPHYSBORO** ZIP CODE **62966**

Motel Murphysboro. IL-13/127 & IL-149 (100 N. 2nd St.) 687-2345.

---

618 AREA CODE   **OKAWVILLE**   ZIP CODE **62271**

Original Mineral Springs Hotel & Bath House. 506 Hanover St., off I-64 & IL-160/177. This is an old hotel, complete with bathhouse, mineral water, whirlpool, steam rooms, massages, swimming pool, and dining. 243-5458.

---

618 AREA CODE   **RED BUD**   ZIP CODE **62278**

English Inn. IL-3 S. 282-3000.

---

618 AREA CODE   **SPARTA**   ZIP CODE **62286**

Mac's Sparta Hotel. IL-4 S (700 S. St. Louis St.). 443-3614.

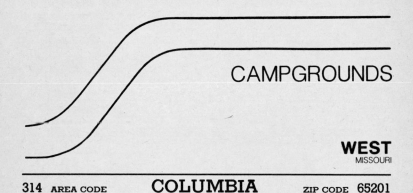

CAMPGROUNDS

WEST
MISSOURI

314 AREA CODE   **COLUMBIA**   ZIP CODE **65201**

Columbia Campground. 500 feet NE of I-70 at U.S. 63 S next to Nickerson Farm Restaurant. All city services offered. Open Mar. 15–Nov. 15. $7.25 per night for two; additional persons extra. 474-2911.

314 AREA CODE   **JONESBURG**   ZIP CODE **63351**

Jonesburg Campground. 58 mi (93.3 km) W of St. Louis on I-70. Exit Jonesburg and go N on Rt. E 1 mi (1.6 km) to campground. Close to Hermann and nearby wineries. Open Jan. 15–Dec. 15. $7 per night for two; additional persons extra. 488-5630.

SOUTHWEST

314 AREA CODE   **TIMES BEACH**   ZIP CODE **63025**

Twin Flags Campground. Go 11 mi (17.7 km) W of I-270 & I-44 and exit westbound Lewis Rd./Times Beach; take N. Outer Rd. W. Cross river, turn left, and travel under interstate to reach S. Outer Road. Turn right on S. Outer Road and go ½ mile. Only 4 mi (6.4 km) to Six Flags. Open year round. $7.50 each night for two; others in party extra. 938-5448.

---

314 AREA CODE   **SULLIVAN**   ZIP CODE **63080**

Sullivan/Meramec Campground. From I-44, take Sullivan exit M-185 S 1 block S to S. Service Rd., then 1 mi (1.6 km) E on S. Service Rd. Near Meramec State Park and Onandaga Cave. Open Mar. 1–Nov. 15. $7.50 per night for two; additional persons extra. 468-8750.

NORTHEAST
ILLINOIS

---

618 AREA CODE   **GRANITE CITY**   ZIP CODE **62040**

Greater St. Louis Campground. From I-270, take IL-3 S, then S to first traffic signal, turn left and go ½ mi (.8 km). Just 15 minutes from downtown St. Louis. Open year round. $6.75 nightly for a party of two; additional persons extra. 931-5160.

---

217 AREA CODE   **SPRINGFIELD**   ZIP CODE **62705**

Springfield Campground. I-55 N or S exit at E. Lake Dr., then follow signs to campground. In the heart of Lincoln Land. Open Apr. 1–Oct. 31. $7.50 per night for two; additional persons extra. 498-7002.

EAST

---

618 AREA CODE   **VANDALIA**   ZIP CODE **62471**

Vandalia Campground. 4 mi (6.4 km) E of Vandalia on I-70 at Brownstown/Bluff City exit (N. Frontage Rd.) near historic Vandalia. Open Mar. 15–Nov. 15. $7 each night for two people; additional persons extra. 427-5140.

SOUTHEAST

---

618 AREA CODE   **BENTON**   ZIP CODE **62812**

Benton Campground. Take exit 71 off I-57 and go 1 block E; at the Pizza Hut turn N and travel 1 mi (1.6 km) on Du Quoin St. Close to Rend Lake. Open year round. $6.50 each night for a party of two; additional persons extra. 439-4860.

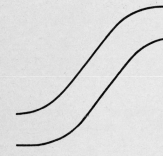

STATE PARKS

In Missouri, all state parks are open
year round. No entrance fee.

NORTHWEST
MISSOURI

Cuivre River State Park. 5 mi (8 km) E of Troy on M-47 in Lincoln
County. Almost 6,000 acres are open to campers, picnickers, and hik-
ers. 314-528-7247.

Graham Cave State Park. In Montgomery County. 2 mi (3.2 km) W of
Danville on Montgomery County Rd. TT from I-70. The travel brochures say the cave was occupied by Indians about 8000 B.C. Campgrounds and trails are available. 314-564-3476.

Mark Twain State Park. In Monroe County on M-107. The focal point
of the 1,192-acre park is the Mark Twain Shrine, housing the cabin
in which Samuel Clemens was born. 314-565-3440.

WEST

Rock Bridge Memorial State Park. 7 mi (11.3 km) S of Columbia and
I-70 on M-163. Devil's Icebox, a cave, is the highlight here. Picnic
sites, a playground, and trails are provided for nonspelunkers. No
camping. 314-449-7402.

SOUTHWEST

Castlewood State Park. On Kiefer Creek Rd., off New Ballwin Rd. &
M-100 (Manchester Rd.) in Castlewood, St. Louis County. Straddling
the Meramec River, the new state park occupies the site of one of
Missouri's premier resort areas of the early 1900s. Picnic sites, a boat

ramp, and a hiking trail are offered, but there is no camping. 314-527-6481.

Dr. Edmund A. Babler Memorial State Park. 20 mi (32.2 km) W of St. Louis on M-109 off St. Louis County Rd. CC. On a 2,445-acre tract, you will find a swimming pool, nature interpretive center, riding stable, picnic areas, and campsites. 314-458-3813.

Elephant Rocks State Park. 4 mi (6.4 km) N of Pilot Knob on M-21 at the NE edge of Graniteville in Iron County. The Elephant Rocks are 1.2 billion years old. The Braille Trail, 1 mi (1.6 km) long, is the first in the state. Picnic facilities available. 314-697-5395.

Hawn State Park. In Ste. Genevieve County between Ste. Genevieve and Farmington on a county road from M-32. On a 10-mi (16.1-km) backpack trail, hike through pine trees and wild azaleas, for which the 2,939-acre park is known. Picnic sites and campsites offered. 314-883-3603.

Johnson's Shut-Ins State Park. 8 mi (12.9 km) N of Lesterville on Reynolds County Rd. M in NE Reynolds County. The E fork of the Black River has, over eons of time, cut canyonlike gaps through a shelf of the oldest exposed rock in Missouri, offering swimmers challenging and exciting routes through the water. Campgrounds are provided, but the park itself operates on a limited-use basis. 314-546-2450.

Meramec State Park. 4 mi (6.4 km) E of Sullivan on M-185 in Franklin County. The park occupies 3,652 acres alongside the Meramec River, making a popular spot for canoers, swimmers, and fishermen. Besides camping facilities, you will find cabins and a dining lodge. Fisher's Cave is open for public tours in the summer. 314-468-6072.

Washington State Park. 14 mi (22.5 km) NE of Potosi on M-21 in Washington County. The Big River borders this 1,415-acre park containing hundreds of petroglyphs, prehistoric carvings in stone, which are interpreted for the public. Complete facilities, including cabins and a dining lodge. 314-586-2995.

NORTHEAST
ILLINOIS

State parks in Illinois are open year round, except New Year's Day and Christmas Day. There is no charge to enter any park.

Beaver Dam State Park. 7 mi (11.3 km) S of Carlinville on a country road between IL 16 & IL 108. This 737-acre park is named in honor of the beaver, which is credited as the original engineer on the park's 59-acre lake. Good facilities for the outdoor enthusiast. Bird watchers will find plenty to observe. 217-854-8020.

Père Marquette State Park. On IL-100 (Great River Rd.) 5 mi (8 km) W of Grafton in Jersey County. A 7,500-acre tract contains bluffs overlooking the nearby confluence of the Mississippi and Illinois rivers. The park's namesake, Father Jacques Marquette, the French Jesuit missionary priest, and Louis Joliet were the first Europeans to enter, in 1673, what is now the state of Illinois at the conjunction of the rivers aforementioned. History abounds within the confines of the park, and there are 18 sites indicating occupation by prehistoric Americans. You can't miss the Père Marquette Lodge, a classic, rustic structure built in the 1930s by members of the Civilian Conservation Corps. Its cabins and rooms are open year round. Meals are served in the lodge. Other facilities include horseback riding, a five-hole golf course, camping, hiking, fishing, and an amphitheater. 618-786-3323 (park info.); 618-786-3351 (lodge).

Sangchris Lake State Park. 18 mi (29 km) SE of Springfield on the New City County Rd. between IL-29 & IL-104. Year-round angling is afforded on this vast waterway warmed by the nearby electrical generators of Commonwealth Edison. The park is situated on 4,055 acres. 217-498-9208.

EAST

Eldon Hazlet State Park. 1351 Ridge St. in Carlyle. Carlyle Lake, 5 mi (8 km) across and 18 mi (29 km) long, draws boaters and sailors, though boat rental is not offered. 10 mi (16.1 km) of roads wind through the park, leading to picnic areas. Camping sites are available to those toting either tent or trailer. 372 sites. 618-594-3015.

South Shore State Park. On the eastern edge of Carlyle Lake (see Eldon Hazlet, above). Camping, picnicking, and boat launches in this 850-acre tract supplement facilities at nearby Eldon Hazlet State Park. Both parks are administered from one office. 33 sites. 618-594-3015.

Stephen A. Forbes State Park. 14 mi (22.5 km) NE of Salem on Omega Rd. off U.S. 50. A 585-acre lake within the 3,019-acre park is well stocked. Boats are available for rent. Campgrounds and hiking trails are open. For pilots, there is a 2,500-foot sod runway for landing small aircraft. 618-547-3381.

SOUTHEAST

Lake Murphysboro State Park. 1 mi (1.6 km) W of Murphysboro off IL-149 in Jackson County. A star-shaped 145-acre lake is bordered by rolling, wooded hills. Orchid-lovers know the 904-acre park features nine types of native Illinois orchids, forming an impressive show of color in Aug. and Sept. Good facilities all around, including an archery range. 618-684-2867.

Pyramid State Park. 6 mi (9.7 km) SW of Pinckneyville off IL-13/127 in Perry County. Heavily forested hills and over two dozen lakes occupy a 2,524-acre site formerly used for strip mining. Fishing, camping, and hiking trails are offered. You will find boat launches at some of the larger lakes. 618-357-2574.

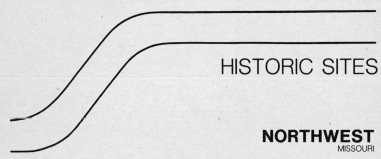

HISTORIC SITES

NORTHWEST
MISSOURI

Mark Twain Birthplace Shrine. In Mark Twain State Park on M-107 in Monroe County near Perry and Paris. In the two-room cabin in which Samuel Clemens was born in 1835, many of Twain's personal items and a library of his books are displayed. 314-565-3449.

Union Covered Bridge. 5 mi (8 km) W of Paris on U.S. 24, then 3 mi (4.8 km) S on Monroe County C and ¼ mi (.4 km) W on gravel road. Missouri's last remaining bridge with a "Burr-arch" truss; constructed in 1870.

Unsinkable Molly Brown House. U.S. 36 at Denkler Alley in Hannibal. Margaret Tobin Brown, known as "Unsinkable Molly Brown," was a famous Hannibal resident. She is credited with saving the lives of many of her fellow passengers on the ill-fated ship *Titanic*, which sank in 1912. Her house has been restored to its 1875 elegance. Closed Nov. through Apr. Admission fee.

For more historic sites, see pp. 5–7.

WEST AND SOUTHWEST

Churchill Memorial. County Rd. F exit off U.S. 54 and turn left on F to Westminster Ave. Turn left again to the corner of 7th St. in Fulton. Housed on the Westminster College Campus, the undercroft of St. Mary Aldermanbury Church houses a museum, gallery and library for the study of Sir Winston Churchill's life. Open daily from 9:45 A.M. Closed holidays. Group rates available. Admission. 314-652-6648.

First State Capitol. 208-216 S. Main St. in the historic district of St. Charles. The focal point of Missouri's government from 1821 to 1826. The building's first floor houses a restored residence and mercantile establishment. Open Mon.–Sat. 10 A.M. to 4 P.M.; noon to 6 P.M. Sundays (Memorial Day to Labor Day); noon to 5 P.M. Sun. the rest of year. 314-723-3256.

Maplewood. M-63 & Rt. AD, Columbia. The 1870 home of Frank G. Nifong is on the National Register of Historic Sites. Open Sun., Apr. through Oct., 2–5 P.M. or by appointment. 314-449-5876.

Newbill-McElhiney House Museum. 625 S. Main St. in St. Charles. This 1838 structure, owned by the St. Charles County Historical Society, has been refurbished and restored to its former grandeur. Open Wednesday through Sunday, 1–4 P.M. No admission fee. 314-723-2939.

Shrine of Our Lady of the Rivers. At the foot of Le Sieur St. in Portage des Sioux. This 27-foot fiberglass statue was erected in gratitude to "Our Lady of the Rivers" in 1951 after the town was saved from the rising floodwaters of the Missouri River. The annual "Blessing of the Fleet" is held here each July. Open daily dawn to dusk.

Sibley Hall. Lindenwood College, Kingshighway, and First Capitol Drive in St. Charles. Lindenwood College, one of the oldest schools west of the Mississippi, was founded in 1827 by Major George C. Sibley and his wife, Mary. The original structure, Sibley Hall, is now the central part of the campus. The college offers tours by appointment only. 314-723-7152.

SOUTHWEST

Moses Austin Grave. Breton St. in Potosi. This plain monument marks the grave of Moses Austin (father of Stephen Austin), who carried out his father's idea of forming a colony in Texas. In 1820 Moses Austin rode to San Antonio and settled 300 American colonists. In poor health, he collapsed and died near Potosi June 10, 1821, on the return journey.

Daniel Boone's Home. M-94 S of St. Louis. Cross Little Femme Osage Creek and take County Rd. F. W to the home. Built between 1803 and 1810, this Georgian structure boasts beautifully carved mantels and woodwork done by Boone himself. The home is open Mar. 15 to Dec. 15, 9:30 A.M. to dusk; weekends only, Dec. 15 to Mar. 15, Camping nearby and museum and gift shop on the grounds. 314-987-2221.

Brinkman House. M-100 W from Hermann. Drive 1½ mi (2.4 km) past the old Eberlin Home to this place. This structure was built in 1855 and is owned by fifth-generation descendants of the original builders.

Fort Davidson State Historic Site. E off M-21 from Pilot Knob onto

County Road V about ¼ mi (.4 km). On Sept. 27, 1864, over 1,000 men (mostly Confederate soldiers) were wounded or killed on this site when an earthen fort was built by Union forces to protect the Iron Mountain and Pilot Knob mineral deposits. An iron marker pinpoints this historic battle.

Deutscheim Historic Site. 109 W. 2nd St. in Hermann. Two historic homes—the Pommer-Gentner House (Market St.) and the Strehly House—are located on this site. The Gentner House reflects Greek revival and Federal architectural influences. The Strehly House was the location of the first print shop in Hermann, where the German-language newspaper *Lichtfreund*, "Friend of Light," was published in the basement. A tour of the Strehly House includes a look at the attached winery, residence, and printshop. Tour reservations should be made a week in advance. Admission fee. 314-486-2200.

Thomas C. Fletcher Home. Elm and 2nd sts. in Hillsboro. This 1½-story log house was built in 1851 by the first native Missourian to serve as governor. The building is maintained by the Jefferson County Park Department, and citizens are now raising money to furnish it. Open by appointment only. 314-789-3911.

German School Museum. 312 Schiller St. in Hermann. This historic spot houses three museums: a children's museum, which includes toys and children's furniture; the River Museum, which memorializes the river men who braved hazardous navigation on the Missouri; and a general museum of artifacts from the Hermann and Gasconade areas. Open daily, Apr. 1 through Nov. 1. Admission fee. 314-486-2017.

The Governor's Mansion. 100 Madison St. in Jefferson City. Constructed in 1871, the mansion has served 29 first families. Public tours given each Mon. and Wed. at 10 and 11 A.M. and 1 P.M. except during Aug. and Dec. and on holidays or when the mansion is in use for official functions. Phone for reservations. 314-751-4141.

Jefferson Landing Historic Site. At the foot of Jefferson St. between the State Capitol and the Governor's Mansion in Jefferson City. This former steamboat landing now contains three restored buildings, including the Lohman Building, which houses a Visitor's Center. Open daily, 8 A.M. to 4:30 P.M. No admission fee. 314-751-3475.

Iron County Courthouse. 250 S. Main, Ironton. This fine example of Greek architecture, a two-story structure, was built in 1858. Union soldiers used it as a refuge when they retreated after the attack on Fort Davidson. Open 9 A.M. to 4 P.M. Mon.-Fri.; 9 A.M. to noon, Sat. 314-586-2811.

Missouri State Museum. First floor of the capitol building in Jefferson City. The History Hall documents Missouri's growth as a state, and the Resources Hall features exhibits on Missouri's natural and man-made resources. Open daily, 8 A.M. to 5 P.M. No admission fee.

Sandy Creek Covered Bridge. 5 mi (8 km) N of Hillsboro on U.S. 21

and 500 feet E on Goldman Rd., which is also Old Lemay Ferry Road. This 76-foot white pine structure is one of only four covered bridges still standing in Missouri. The bridge was built in 1872 and rebuilt in 1887 and 1940, and it still carries traffic.

The Schilling-Saunders Home. ¾ mi (1.2 km) W of M-19 near Hermann at Sawmill Rd. and 1 mi (1.6 km) N on the right (see map). This home was built in the 1840s to support extensive vineyards and winemaking by the Schilling family.

St. Joachim's Catholic Church. On M-21 just inside Old Mines, Mo. This simple and beautiful historic brick church was built in 1828. Services are held Mon. through Sat. at 8:30 A.M., Sat. evening at 5 P.M., and Sun. at 7, 9, and 11 A.M.

St. John's Church. E of Fredericksburg on County Road J. This beautiful stone chapel, built over 100 years ago, is still actively serving the community. In 1978 the West German Broadcasting Company selected this congregation and church as the subject of a film on Missouri's German Heritage.

St. Joseph's Church. Main St., Westphalia. This majestic church houses stained-glass windows from Germany, elegant wrought-iron hinges and massive doors, and an organ that is known throughout the world. 314-455-2320.

State Capitol Building. Jefferson City. The grand stairway here is said to be one of the widest staircases in the world. The huge bronze door is reputed to be among the largest built in this century. Free guided tours every half hour from 8 A.M. to 4 P.M. during the week and every hour on the hour on weekends. 314-751-4127.

NORTHEAST

Elijah Lovejoy Monument. 5th St. and Monument Ave. in the Alton Cemetery. A tribute to the abolitionist editor who lost his life to an angry mob when he tried to protect his press.

Lincoln-Douglas Debate Marker. E. Broadway at Market St. The last debate between these two famous statesmen was held in the Alton City Hall, which stood at this site.

Mansion House. 506 State St. in Alton. Built in 1834, this home served for 100 years as a lodging house. Although the house is not open to visitors today, it's still worth driving by to note the nineteenth-century charm.

Colonel Samuel Buckmaster House. 514 State St. in Alton. This three-story house was built between 1835 and 1850 and was owned by Col. Samuel Buckmaster, who served as the mayor of Alton in 1853 and again in 1862. The house is not open to the public.

Illinois State Capitol. 2nd and Capitol sts. in Springfield. This is the current home of the Illinois legislature. Begun in 1867 and completed in 1888, the building houses murals and bas-reliefs. This first floor is open daily; guided tours available. No admission fee. 217-782-2099. (Springfield offers many more historic sites to visit. For a full listing see p. 85.)

EAST

William Jennings Bryan Home and Museum. 408 S. Broadway in Salem. The three-time Democratic presidential nominee was born in this two-story frame house March 19, 1860. His home is now a museum filled with memorabilia. Open Sat. through Wed. Admission fee. No phone.

Cahokia Mounds. 7850 Collinsville Rd. 5 mi (8 km) E of St. Louis. Early Illinois Indians once worshiped at what is now believed to be the largest collection of earthwork monuments in North America. 618-344-5268.

Vandalia Statehouse. 315 Gallatin St. in Vandalia. For 20 years this was the site of Illinois' state capitol during the early 1800s. Tours are given here and include a look at the starkly furnished Supreme Court Room and the treasurer's office. Open daily 9 A.M. to 5 P.M. No admission fee. 618-283-1161.

SOUTHEAST

Cahokia Courthouse. 1st & Elm sts. in Cahokia. This structure, built in the mid-1700s, is thought to be the oldest house in Illinois. It became the courthouse in 1793 and, at one time, it was the seat of government for the Northwest Territory. 618-332-1782.

Fort de Chartres. Fort de Chartres State Historic Site, 4 mi (6.4 km) W of Prairie du Rocher. Walls 4 feet thick and 18 feet high enclosed King Louis XV's once fortified French outpost in the New World. Today the old fort features a rebuilt guardhouse, gatehouses, and the original foundation of the officers' quarters. Buy handcrafted pioneer goods at the trading post. A "Rendezvous," held the first weekend each June, is an invitation to participate in activities commonly enjoyed during the fort's early days. Open daily, 9 A.M. to 5 P.M. No admission fee. 618-284-7230. (See also *La Pelleterie,* p. 125.)

Governor Daniel Dunklin's Grave. Located on Dunklin Drive in Herculaneum, overlooking the Mississippi River. Dunklin, Missouri's fifth governor from 1832 to 1836, is credited with establishing the state's public school system.

Kaskaskia and Kaskaskia Bell. On Kaskaskia Island, which can be reached by crossing the toll bridge (M-51) at Chester and turning N on County Rd. H to the town of St. Mary's, Missouri. The site of Old Kaskaskia, a town that was abandoned in 1881 after repeated river floodings. Today there is a memorial shrine where the village once stood. Inside you will find the bell that once hung in the Kaskaskia church steeple. The bell was cast in Paris in 1741 and was given to the Kaskaskia parish by Louis XV. The bell, known as the "Liberty Bell of the West," has a resemblance to its eastern sister: it is also cracked.

Fort Kaskaskia Historic Site. Just off IL-3 near Chester. This historic area overlooks the confluence of the Mississippi and Kaskaskia rivers. This was once the site of the old French fort of Kaskaskia, built in 1736, rebuilt in 1761, and then destroyed in 1767 to prevent British occupation. Garrison Hill and Menard cemeteries, both located here, contain the remains of 3,800 bodies that were moved from Kaskaskia Island during the flood of 1881. Camping available. No admission fee.

Pierre Menard Home. Just past Fort Kaskaskia Historic Site off IL-3 near Chester. Illinois' first lieutenant governor built his stately French colonial home here. Each January, on the first or second Sunday, a French Yule bash with dancing, colonial food, and costumes is celebrated at the home. Open daily 9 A.M. to 5 P.M. year round. No admission fee. 618-859-3031.

The Felix Valle Home. On the corner of Merchant and 2nd sts. in Ste. Genevieve. Built in 1818, the American Federal-style home was purchased in 1824 by Jean B. Valle. It served as headquarters for Menard and Valle, a company that controlled Indian trade throughout Missouri and Arkansas. 314-883-7102. (For a complete listing of historic sites in Ste. Genevieve see p. 127.)

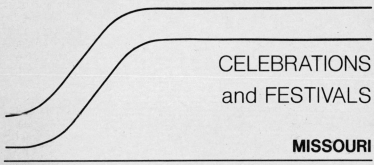

CELEBRATIONS
and FESTIVALS

MISSOURI

MARCH

Wurstfest. A winter break featuring the best "wurst" there is—the edible kind—in the "Sausage Capital of Missouri." First full weekend. Hermann. 314-486-2030.

St. Pat's Celebration. The patron saint of engineers is honored in festivities at the University of Missouri—Rolla. Weekend prior to St. Pat's Day, or in the event the Day of Green falls on the weekend itself, it is held that weekend. Rolla. 314-341-4259.

Missouri Whitewater Championships. The Arnold Whitewater Association sponsors a nonprofit race for the thrill of both racers and spectators on Missouri's fastest stream. Second, third, or fourth weekend, depending on water conditions. Silvermines Campground in Mark Twain National Forest, Hwy. D and St. Francis River near Fredericktown. 314-726-0656.

MAY

Hermannfest. Entertainment for all ages in a springtime affair. First two weekends. Hermann. 314-486-2313.

Maifest. German is the theme in dance, music, costume, and food as a German May Festival takes place in Hermann. Winery and house tours. Third weekend. 314-486-2017.

JUNE

Jefferson County Championship Rodeo. Cowboys compete for top-dollar prize money as they ride and rope their way through this event. Live entertainment is also held at the show grounds. Hillsboro. 314-937-7697.

Summer Festival. Held at the beginning of June in Kimmswick. Activities range from arts and crafts demonstrations to square dancing and a greased-pig-catching contest. You can also tour the restored homes of Kimmswick. Admission fee. 314-467-3020.

Riverfest. River excursions, arts and crafts, music, and a catfish barbecue reflect the influences of the Muddy Mississippi on a river town. Third weekend. Cape Girardeau. 314-335-3312.

JULY

Hillsboro Horse Show and Festival. Horse owners compete in this five-day event that features carnival rides, crafts, food, and a beer tent. 314-789-2600.

National Tom Sawyer Fence Painting Contest. Mark Twain's boyhood home is the site of this contest; held during the culmination of Tom Sawyer Days. Check out the frog jumping, raft racing, and fireworks too. July 4 holiday. Hannibal. 314-221-2477.

Family Bluegrass Music Weekend. Foot-stomping is in order as bluegrass bands and fans gather. Fourth weekend. At Sam A. Baker State Park in Patterson. 314-751-2479.

AUGUST

Grape Stomping Festival. Take off your shoes and hop in. First full weekend. At Stone Hill Winery in Hermann. 314-486-2221.

Jour de Fête. Ste. Genevieve comes forth with its French heritage in a street festival of folk dancing, food, and arts and crafts galore. Second weekend. 314-883-5609.

SEPTEMBER

St. James Grape & Fall Festival. A harvesttime version of a county fair. Weekend following Labor Day. At the St. James Community Fairgrounds in St. James. 314-265-8294.

OCTOBER

Octoberfest. Samplings of the bottled grapes go well with German food, song, and dance. Every weekend. At the Stone Hill Winery in Hermann. 314-486-2221.

Apple Butter Festival. Homemade apple butter and tours of the restored homes are the highlights of this event. Last weekend in October. Kimmswick. Admission fee. 314-467-3020.

NOVEMBER

Autumn Folklife Festival. Blacksmiths, pewter casters, and basket makers are showcased, along with food, music, street theater, and children's games, all reflecting the culture of Missouri and the Hannibal area. First weekend. In Hannibal's Historic District. 314-221-6545.

DECEMBER

Candelight Tour. Held the first Sunday in December in Kimmswick to celebrate the Christmas season. The restored homes of Kimmswick are decorated, and guides dress in period costumes during the tour. There is a tour fee. 314-467-3020.

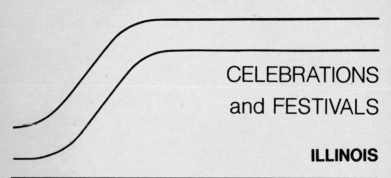

CELEBRATIONS
and FESTIVALS

ILLINOIS

JANUARY

Twelfth Night. Dancing, colonial food and costumed entertainers at the Pierre Menard Home on the French Yule. First or second Sunday, at the home located past the Fort Kaskaskia Historic Site on IL-3 outside of Chester, Ill. 618-859-3031.

FEBRUARY

Maple Syrup Time. Learn the step-by-step process for a sweet taste test. Lincoln's Birthday through the end of February. At Lincoln Memorial Gardens in Springfield. 217-529-1111.

JUNE

Fort de Chartres Rendezvous. A return to the days of yore with tomahawk-throwing buckskinned militia battles and fife and drum corps at King Louis XV's once-fortified outpost. First weekend. Prairie du Rocher. 618-284-7230.

Grand Levee. Candlelight tours of the restored capitol where Lincoln started his career. Second weekend. Vandalia. 618-283-1161.

Farm and Folk Festival. DuQuoin Fairgrounds at the end of June. Crafts, food and the Illinois Championship Cow Chip Tossing Contest are highlights. 618-542-5484.

AUGUST

Illinois State Fair. First two weeks of the month. Springfield. 312-793-2094.

DuQuoin State Fair. Last weekend through Labor Day. DuQuoin. 618-542-5484.

SEPTEMBER

Apple Festival. Illinois' biggest. Parades, dancing and marching bands, all in honor of the crunchy red fruit. Second week. Murphysboro. 618-684-3811 or 684-6421.

NOVEMBER

Way of Lights. The Nativity comes to light at night in an unusual display of outdoor sculpture. Day after Thanksgiving through the first week of January. At Our Lady of the Snows National Shrine in Belleville. 618-397-6700.

Annual Christmas Walk. Gifts and crafts. Third week in November. Marissa.

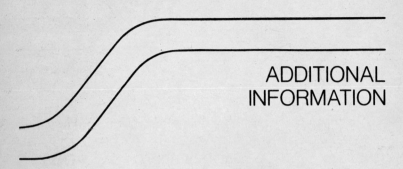

ADDITIONAL INFORMATION

Daytrippers who are especially interested in visiting arts and crafts fairs may obtain a statewide listing of such events by sending a $1 donation to:

Craft Alliance
6640 Delmar Blvd.
St. Louis, MO 63130
Attn: Missouri Craft and Art Fairs (for current year)

For those who want information on historic preservation, you may obtain a statewide listing of tours, festivals, and events by writing to:

Illinois Department of Conservation
Division of Historic Sites
405 East Washington St.
Springfield, IL 62706
Attn: Illinois Preservation Calendar (for current year)

For a six-month statewide calendar of events write to:

Illinois Office of Tourism
222 South College St.
Springfield, IL 62706
Attn: Illinois Calendar of Events

TRAVEL INFORMATION

AMTRAK ROUTES

If traveling by train is a consideration, call or write Amtrak for current scheduling information. From all points in Missouri, call 800-621-0317. From Illinois, dial 800-572-2419. The St. Louis Amtrak station is situated at 550 South 16th Street, St. Louis, Missouri, 63103. Established routes exist between St. Louis and Kansas City, and between St. Louis and Chicago, with selected stops along the way. All schedules, however, are subject to change. Deaf persons with access to a teletypewriter should call 800-523-6590 (or 6591) to receive information and make reservations via Amtrak's teletypewriter service.

GREYHOUND ROUTES

If you wish to travel by bus, call or write Greyhound for current scheduling information. From its ticket office and depot, Greyhound encompasses motor coach service for both Gulf Transport and Great Southern Coaches lines. The Greyhound Bus Depot is situated at 801 North Broadway, St. Louis, Missouri, 63102; it is reached by dialing 314-231-7800. All schedules are subject to change. For the hearing-impaired, Greyhound's Silent Information Service is reached by telephoning 800-345-3109. Many routes are express to major points of destination only.